Volume X
Publication No. 103
November 1978

Self-Involvement in the Middle East Conflict

Formulated by the
Committee on International Relations

Group for the Advancement of Psychiatry

This publication was produced for the Group for the Advancement of Psychiatry by the Mental Health Materials Center, Inc., New York.

Additional copies of this GAP Publication No. 103 are available at the following prices: 1–9 copies, $6.00 each; 10–24 copies, list less 15 percent; 25–99 copies, list less 20 percent; 100–499 copies, list less 30 percent.

Upon request the Publications Office of the Group for the Advancement of Psychiatry will provide a complete listing of GAP titles currently in print, quantity prices, and information on subscriptions assuring the receipt of new publications as they are released.

Orders amounting to less than $5.00 must be accompanied by remittance. All prices are subject to change without notice.

Please send your order and remittance to: Publications Office, Group for the Advancement of Psychiatry, 419 Park Avenue South, New York, New York 10016.

Library of Congress Cataloging in Publication Data

Group for the Advancement of Psychiatry. Committee on International Relations.

Self-Involvement in the Middle East Conflict.

(Publication—Group for the Advancement of Psychiatry; v. 10, no. 103)
Includes bibliographical references.

1. Jewish-Arab relations—Psychological aspects. 2. Palestinian Arabs—Psychology. 3. Israelis—Psychology. 4. Narcissism. I. Title. II. Series: Group for the Advancement of Psychiatry. Publication—Group for the Advancement of Psychiatry; no. 103.

DS119.7.G74 1978   956'.04'019   78–12608
ISBN 0–87318–140–9

Printed in the United States of America

TABLE OF CONTENTS

This is the fourth in a series of publications comprising Volume X. For a list of other GAP
publications on topics of current interest, see last page of book herein.

STATEMENT OF PURPOSE

THE GROUP FOR THE ADVANCEMENT OF PSYCHIATRY has a membership of approximately 300 psychiatrists, most of whom are organized in the form of a number of working committees. These committees direct their efforts toward the study of various aspects of psychiatry and the application of this knowledge to the fields of mental health and human relations.

Collaboration with specialists in other disciplines has been and is one of GAP's working principles. Since the formation of GAP in 1946 its members have worked closely with such other specialists as anthropologists, biologists, economists, statisticians, educators, lawyers, nurses, psychologists, sociologists, social workers, and experts in mass communication, philosophy, and semantics. GAP envisages a continuing program of work according to the following aims:

1. To collect and appraise significant data in the fields of psychiatry, mental health, and human relations
2. To reevaluate old concepts and to develop and test new ones
3. To apply the knowledge thus obtained for the promotion of mental health and good human relations

GAP is an independent group, and its reports represent the composite findings and opinions of its members only, guided by its many consultants.

SELF-INVOLVEMENT IN THE MIDDLE EAST CONFLICT was formulated by the Committee on International Relations which acknowledges on page 390 the participation of others in the preparation of this report. The members of this committee are listed below. The following pages list the members of the other GAP committees as well as additional membership categories and current and past officers of GAP.

COMMITTEE ON INTERNATIONAL RELATIONS

Ronald M. Wintrob, Farmington, CT, Chairman
Francis F. Barnes, Chevy Chase, MD
*Robert N. Dorn, Virginia Beach, VA
John E. Mack, Chestnut Hill, MA
*David N. Ratnavale, Virginia Beach, VA
Rita R. Rogers, Torrance, CA
Bertram H. Schaffner, New York, NY
*Stephen B. Shanfield, Tucson, AZ
Mottram P. Torre, New Orleans, LA
Bryant M. Wedge, Washington, DC
Roy M. Whitman, Cincinnati, OH

* Though participating as guests during formulation of this report, they have since become full members of the committee.

COMMITTEE ON ADOLESCENCE

Warren J. Gadpaille, Englewood, CO,
Chairman
Sherman C. Feinstein, Highland Park, IL
Maurice R. Friend, New York, NY
Charles A. Malone, Cleveland, OH
Derek Miller, Chicago, IL
Silvio J. Onesti, Jr., Belmont, MA

COMMITTEE ON AGING

Prescott W. Thompson, San Jose, CA,
Chairman
Gene D. Cohen, Rockville, MD
Charles M. Gaitz, Houston, TX
Lawrence F. Greenleigh, Los Angeles, CA
Maurice E. Linden, Philadelphia, PA
Robert D. Patterson, Lexington, MA
Eric Pfeiffer, Denver, CO
F. Conyers Thompson, Jr., Atlanta, GA
Jack Weinberg, Chicago, IL

COMMITTEE ON CHILD PSYCHIATRY

Joseph Fischhoff, Detroit, MI,
Chairman
Paul L. Adams, Louisville, KY
E. James Anthony, St. Louis, MO
James M. Bell, Canaan, NY
Harold Donald Dunton, New York, NY
Joseph M. Green, Madison, WI
John F. Kenward, Chicago, IL
Ake Mattsson, Pittsburgh, PA
John F. McDermott, Jr., Honolulu, HI
Theodore Shapiro, New York, NY
Exie E. Welsch, New York, NY
Virginia N. Wilking, New York, NY

COMMITTEE ON THE COLLEGE STUDENT

Malkah Tolpin Notman, Brookline, MA,
Chairman
Robert L. Arnstein, Hamden, CT
Harrison P. Eddy, New York, NY
Varda Peller Ganz, LaJolla, CA
Myron B. Liptzin, Chapel Hill, NC
Gloria C. Onque, Pittsburgh, PA
Elizabeth Aub Reid, Cambridge, MA
Kent E. Robinson, Towson, MD

Earle Silber, Chevy Chase, MD
Tom G. Stauffer, White Plains, NY

COMMITTEE ON THE FAMILY

Joseph Satten, San Francisco, CA,
Chairman
C. Christian Beels, New York, NY
Ivan Boszormenyi-Nagy, Wyncote, PA
Murray Bowen, Chevy Chase, MD
Henry U. Grunebaum, Cambridge, MA
Margaret M. Lawrence, Pomona, NY
David Mendell, Houston, TX
Carol Nadelson, Boston, MA
Norman L. Paul, Boston, MA

COMMITTEE ON GOVERNMENTAL AGENCIES

Sidney S. Goldensohn, Jamaica, NY,
Chairman
William S. Allerton, Richmond, VA
Albert M. Biele, Philadelphia, PA
Roger Peele, Washington, DC
Marvin E. Perkins, Fincastle, VA
Harvey Lee Ruben, New Haven, CT
William W. Van Stone, Palo Alto, CA

COMMITTEE ON MEDICAL EDUCATION

Paul Tyler Wilson, Bethesda, MD,
Chairman
David R. Hawkins, Charlottesville, VA
Harold I. Lief, Philadelphia, PA
Herbert Pardes, Englewood, CO
Jeanne Spurlock, Silver Spring, MD
Bryce Templeton, Philadelphia, PA
Sidney L. Werkman, Denver, CO
Sherwyn M. Woods, Los Angeles, CA

COMMITTEE ON MENTAL HEALTH SERVICES

Allan Beigel, Tucson, AZ,
Chairman
Mary Ann B. Bartusis, Philadelphia, PA
Eugene M. Caffey, Jr., Washington, DC
Merrill T. Eaton, Omaha, NB
Joseph T. English, New York, NY
James B. Funkhouser, Richmond, VA
Robert S. Garber, Belle Mead, NJ

COMMITTEE ON PUBLIC EDUCATION

Robert J. Campbell, New York, NY,
  Chairman
James A. Knight, New Orleans, LA
Norman L. Loux, Sellersville, PA
Mildred Mitchell-Bateman, Charleston, WV
Mabel Ross, Sun City, AZ
Julius Schreiber, Washington, DC
Robert H. Sharpley, Cambridge, MA
Miles F. Shore, Boston, MA
Robert A. Solow, Beverly Hills, CA
Kent A. Zimmerman, Berkeley, CA

COMMITTEE ON RESEARCH

Jerry M. Lewis, Dallas, TX
  Chairman
John E. Adams, Gainesville, FL
Robert Cancro, New York, NY
Stanley H. Eldred, Belmont, MA
John G. Gunderson, Belmont, MA
Morris A. Lipton, Chapel Hill, NC
John G. Looney, Dallas, TX
Ralph R. Notman, Brookline, MA
Charles P. O'Brien, Philadelphia, PA
Alfred H. Stanton, Wellesley Hills, MA
John S. Strauss, New Haven, CT
Gene L. Usdin, New Orleans, LA
Herbert Weiner, Bronx, NY

COMMITTEE ON SOCIAL ISSUES

Roy W. Menninger, Topeka, KS,
  Chairman
Henry J. Gault, Highland Park, IL
Roderic Gorney, Los Angeles, CA
Lester Grinspoon, Boston, MA
Joel S. Handler, Evanston, IL
Perry Ottenberg, Merion Station, PA
Kendon W. Smith, Piermont, NY

COMMITTEE ON THERAPEUTIC CARE

Thomas E. Curtis, Chapel Hill, NC,
  Chairman
Bernard Bandler, Cambridge, MA
Andrea K. Delgado, New York, NY
Robert W. Gibson, Towson, MD
Harold A. Greenberg, Silver Spring, MD
Donald W. Hammersley, Washington, DC

Roberto L. Jimenez, Newton Center, MA
Milton Kramer, Cincinnati, OH
Orlando B. Lightfoot, Boston, MA
Melvin Sabshin, Washington, DC
Benjamin Simon, Boston, MA
Robert E. Switzer, Trevose, PA

COMMITTEE ON THERAPY

Robert Michels, New York, NY,
  Chairman
Henry W. Brosin, Tucson, AZ
Eugene B. Feigelson, New York, NY
Tokoz Byram Karasu, New York, NY
Andrew P. Morrison, Cambridge, MA
William Offenkrantz, Chicago, IL,
Franz K. Reichsman, Brooklyn, NY
Lewis L. Robbins, Glen Oaks, NY
Allan D. Rosenblatt, La Jolla, CA
Justin Simon, Berkeley, CA

CONTRIBUTING MEMBERS

Carlos C. Alden, Jr., Buffalo, NY
Charlotte G. Babcock, Pittsburgh, PA
Grace Baker, New York, NY
Spencer Bayles, Houston, TX
Aaron T. Beck, Wynnewood, PA
Sidney Berman, Washington, DC
H. Waldo Bird, St. Louis, MO
Wilfred Bloomberg, Cambridge, MA
Thomas L. Brannick, Imola, CA
H. Keith H. Brodie, Durham, NC
Eugene Brody, Baltimore, MD
Ewald W. Busse, Durham, NC
Dale C. Cameron, San Diego, CA
Ian L. W. Clancey, Ontario, Canada
Sanford I. Cohen, Boston, MA
Robert Coles, Cambridge, MA
Frank J. Curran, New York, NY
William D. Davidson, Washington, DC
Lloyd C. Elam, Nashville, TN
Louis C. English, Pomona, NY
Stuart M. Finch, Tucson, AZ
Alfred Flarsheim, Chicago, IL
Archie R. Foley, New York, NY
Alan Frank, Albuquerque, NM
Daniel X. Freedman, Chicago, IL
Albert J. Glass, San Francisco, CA
Louis A. Gottschalk, Irvine, CA

Alexander Gralnick, Port Chester, NY
Milton Greenblatt, Los Angeles, CA
Maurice H. Greenhill, Rye, NY
John H. Greist, Indianapolis, IN
Roy R. Grinker, Sr., Chicago, IL
Ernest M. Gruenberg, Baltimore, MD
Stanley Hammons, Tuscaloosa, AL
Saul I. Harrison, Ann Arbor, MI
Mary O'Neill Hawkins, New York, NY
J. Cotter Hirschberg, Topeka, KS
Edward J. Hornick, New York, NY
Joseph Hughes, Philadelphia, PA
Portia Bell Hume, Berkeley, CA
Benjamin Jeffries, Harper Woods, MI
*Irene M. Josselyn, Phoenix, AZ
Jay Katz, New Haven, CT
Sheppard G. Kellam, Chicago, IL
Donald F. Klein, New York, NY
Gerald L. Klerman, Rockville, MD
Peter H. Knapp, Boston, MA
Othilda M. Krug, Cincinnati, OH
*John P. Lambert, Katonah, NY
Zigmond M. Lebensohn, Washington, DC
Henry D. Lederer, Washington, DC
Robert L. Leopold, Philadelphia, PA
Alan I. Levenson, Tucson, AZ
Earl A. Loomis, Jr., Greenport, NY
Reginald S. Lourie, Chevy Chase, MD
Alfred O. Ludwig, Boston, MA
Jeptha R. MacFarlane, Garden City, NY
John A. MacLeod, Cincinnati, OH
Sidney G. Margolin, Englewood, CO
Peter A. Martin, Southfield, MI
Mary E. Mercer, Nyack, NY
Eugene Meyer, Baltimore, MD
James G. Miller, Louisville, KY
John E. Nardini, Bethesda, MD
Peter B. Neubauer, New York, NY
Joseph D. Noshpitz, Washington, DC
Lucy D. Ozarin, Bethesda, MD
Bernard L. Pacella, New York, NY
William L. Peltz, Manchester, VT
Irving Philips, San Francisco, CA
Charles A. Pinderhughes, Bedford, MA
Harvey L. P. Resnik, College Park, MD
Milton Rosenbaum, Bronx, NY
W. Donald Ross, Cincinnati, OH
Lester H. Rudy, Chicago, IL

George E. Ruff, Philadelphia, PA
David S. Sanders, Beverly Hills, CA
Kurt O. Schlesinger, San Francisco, CA
Robert A. Senescu, Albuquerque, NM
Calvin F. Settlage, Sausalito, CA
Richard I. Shader, Newton Center, MA
Harley C. Shands, New York, NY
Albert J. Silverman, Ann Arbor, MI
Benson R. Snyder, Cambridge, MA
John P. Spiegel, Waltham, MA
Brandt F. Steele, Denver, CO
Eleanor A. Steele, Denver, CO
Rutherford B. Stevens, New York, NY
Alan A. Stone, Cambridge, MA
Perry C. Talkington, Dallas, TX
Graham C. Taylor, Montreal, Canada
Harvey J. Tompkins, New York, NY
Lucia E. Tower, Chicago, IL
Joseph P. Tupin, Sacramento, CA
Montague Ullman, Ardsley, NY
Suzanne T. van Amerongen, Cambridge, MA
Robert S. Wallerstein, San Francisco, CA
Andrew S. Watson, Ann Arbor, MI
Edward M. Weinshel, San Francisco, CA
Joseph B. Wheelwright, Kentfield, CA
Robert L. Williams, Houston, TX
Stanley F. Yolles, Stony Brook, NY
Israel Zwerling, Philadelphia, PA

LIFE MEMBERS

S. Spafford Ackerly, Louisville, KY
Kenneth E. Appel, Ardmore, PA
Leo H. Bartemeier, Baltimore, MD
Walter E. Barton, Hartland, VT
Ivan C. Berlien, Coral Gables, FL
O. Spurgeon English, Narberth, PA
Dana L. Farnsworth, Belmont, MA
Edward O. Harper, Cleveland, OH
Marion E. Kenworthy, New York, NY
Karl A. Menninger, Topeka, KS
Benjamin Simon, Boston, MA
Francis A. Sleeper, Cape Elizabeth, ME

LIFE CONSULTANT

Mrs. Ethel L. Ginsburg, New York, NY

*deceased

COMMITTEE ACKNOWLEDGMENTS

The Committee on International Relations gratefully acknowledges its indebtedness to members, fellows, guests and consultants who assisted us in formulating this report.

Members who participated in planning and research in early phases of the study are the late John A. P. Millet, M.D., the late Frank Fremont-Smith, M.D., Eugene B. Brody, M.D., William D. Davidson, M.D., and Robert L. Leopold, M.D. Eric Baum, M.D., made numerous valuable contributions to the study and to this report during his tenure as a member of the Committee. Fellows who contributed richly have been Mauricio Cortina, M.D., Robert E. Nadeau, M.D. and Charles C. Rohrs, M.D. Robert Cancro, M.D., Leah Davidson, M.D., Robert M. Dorn, M.D., David N. Ratnavale, M.D., and Stephen B. Shanfield, M.D. provided valuable insights as psychiatrist-guests of the Committee.

Several consultants provided invaluable perspectives into the problems of sorting out and assessing psychological factors in a multi-dimensional arena of human transactions. We are grateful to Thomas Kuhn of Princeton University for his perspectives into the scientific process, to Edward T. Hall of Northwestern University for assistance with the factors of culture and culture conflict, to Dieter Senghaas of Harvard and Goethe University of Frankfort-Main for his appreciation of the dynamics of the international system, to Muzafer Sherif of Pennsylvania State University for increasing our awareness of the potency of group processes, and to Abid A. Al-Marayati of the University of Toledo for his counsel concerning the political process in the Middle East and the Arab outlook on this.

Many people among the societies of the Middle East provided extensive and thoughtful discussions of their own involvements in the conflicts of their nations. And several knowledgeable scholars of the history and politics of the region reviewed the manuscript for factual accuracy. Any errors that remain are our own.

The Committee began its deliberations on self-involvement in the conflicts of nations under the chairmanship of Bryant Wedge, M.D., who continued to guide the work of the Committee from the early stages of discussion in 1972 until the drafting of the report in 1977. Ronald Wintrob, M.D., assumed the chairmanship of the Committee in 1977.

The Committee also acknowledges the editorial assistance of Mrs. Peggy Yntema in the preparation of this report.

Editor's note:

The maps on the following pages will facilitate the reader in identifying the area in dispute. They have been adapted from *The Middle East & the New Realism,* a Special Report of the International Peace Academy (777 United Nations Plaza, New York, NY 10017) by Indar Rikhye and John Volkmar, 1975. Used by permission of the publisher.

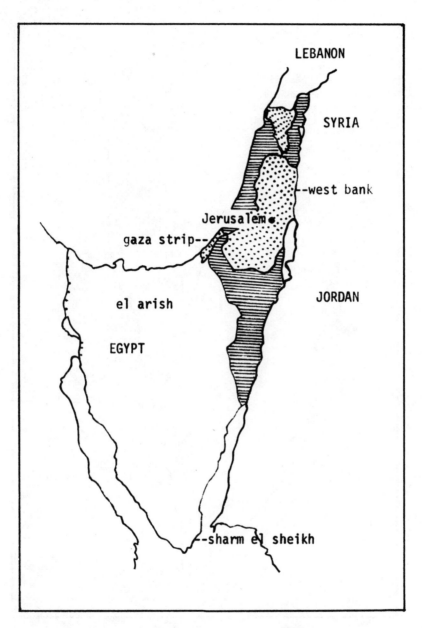

LEBANON

SYRIA

--west bank

Jerusalem

gaza strip--

el arish

EGYPT

JORDAN

--sharm el sheikh

1947 U.N. PARTITION PLAN

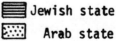

Jewish state

Arab state

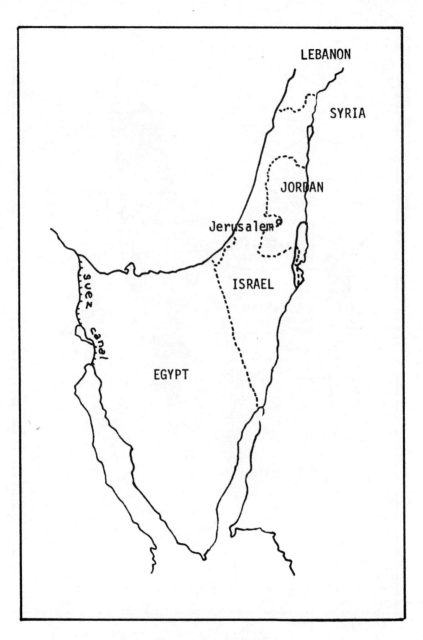

ISRAEL BEFORE 1967

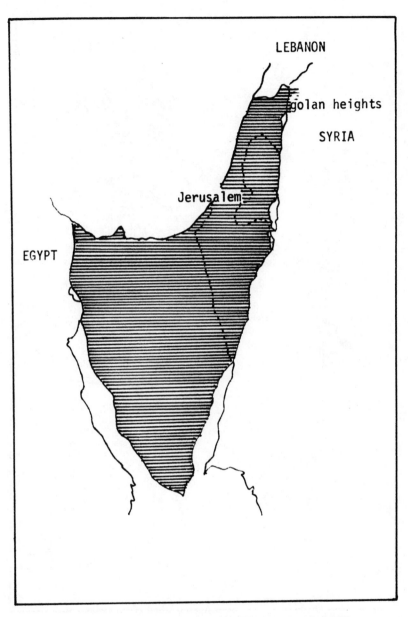

LEBANON

golan heights

SYRIA

Jerusalem

EGYPT

ISRAEL & OCCUPIED TERRITORIES 1967-1973

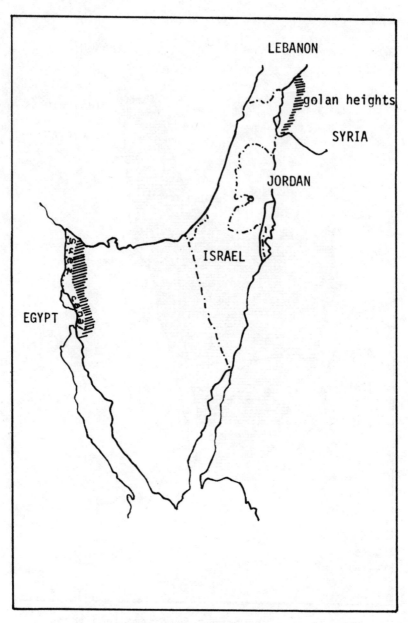

LEBANON

golan heights

SYRIA

JORDAN

ISRAEL

EGYPT

U.N. BUFFER ZONES AFTER OCTOBER 1973 ▤

INTRODUCTION

War is the critical manifestation of international and civil conflict and a crucial problem for mankind in the twentieth century. While the principal actors in the institution of war are nations or national-states, any theory of war must account for the willingness of individual citizens to participate in this activity of the nation. The unit of analysis on which this Committee determined it could most fruitfully focus its attention in considering war behavior is the individual human actor in relation to conditions of international conflict. We do not consider that psychic states are the "cause" of war. War is too complex a social institution to attribute its cause to any one dimension or factor. However, since war requires the involvement of great numbers of individuals, our question is: What elements of human psychology contribute to individual willingness to support and participate in the wars of nations? What psychological states predispose to war?

The focus of this report is the participation of individuals in the conflicts of nations. In particular, we examine the impact of national conflict in the international arena on the individual's self-system. We have chosen to study citizen-participants in the protracted Middle East conflict, examined in the light of recent developments in clinical and theoretical appreciation of the role of the self in personal behavior, particularly personal aggression. We propose and commence to explore the hypothesis that *real or imagined threat or injury to the nation may be perceived by the individual as a danger or humiliation to the self,* and that individual response to such events is substantially rooted in the distinctive psychological dynamics of the self and its extension.

Background of the study

The Committee on International Relations was formed in 1947; its first Report on THE POSITION OF PSYCHIATRISTS IN

395

THE FIELD OF INTERNATIONAL RELATIONS (GAP Report No. 11) was issued in January 1950 and advocated, among other items, ". . . emphasizing . . . the importance of psychological considerations in the planning and implementation of international policies . . ." Subsequent studies have been concerned with WORKING ABROAD: A DISCUSSION OF PSYCHOLOGICAL ATTITUDES AND ADAPTATION IN NEW SITUATIONS (GAP Report No. 41, 1958), APPLICATION OF PSYCHIATRIC INSIGHTS TO CROSS-CULTURAL COMMUNICATION (GAP Symposium No. 7, 1961) and THE PSYCHIATRIST AND PUBLIC ISSUES (GAP Report No. 74, 1969). In addition, the Committee has participated in such studies as PSYCHIATRIC ASPECTS OF THE PREVENTION OF NUCLEAR WAR (GAP Report No. 57, 1964) and METHODS OF FORCEFUL INDOCTRINATION (GAP Symposium No. 4, 1957), as well as a number of explorations of related topics. Throughout its history, the Committee has recognized war and war behavior as a central issue in its field of concern. It has returned to the issue again and again, approaching it from various levels of analysis in terms of emerging understanding of psychological factors.

This report represents the Committee's first essay in the field; it grew out of recognition that our methods are best suited to studying the role of individual psychology and our conviction that this somehow plays a part in the war behavior of nations in the international system. In reviewing current explanations of war behavior, we found that general theories of human aggression and mass aggression are thoroughly unsatisfactory in explaining individual participation; we found it necessary to approach the problem empirically and clinically. We decided to examine as directly as possible the participation of individual actors in the conflicts of their nations.

As noted in the acknowledgment, a number of psychiatrists have directly participated in the study, each seeking direct contact with involved individuals. We chose the Middle

East conflict as the most active and war-prone case available. We began to compare our observations with hypotheses about the roots of war behavior.

Four general explanations for human aggressivity may be distinguished: *evolutionary-instinctual* drives are expressed in patterns of behavior; *learned behavioral* patterns are associated with institutionalized expectations; *aggressive response* patterns are activated by frustration; and *aggressive psychopathological* manifestations are the outcome of personality disturbances. Without attempting to assess the relative roles of these factors or to reconcile their relationship, we propose as a result of this study to add a fifth explanation: *the potential for violence in the reaction of the self to injury or threat to cohesion and continuity, whether experienced in its core or in its extensions.* We emphasize that the "psychological defense of self"* is a distinctively and exclusively human activity that can be studied only in terms of individual human behavior.

The method of study

When we began this study in 1972, the Middle East had been the site of three wars in less than a quarter century; the armistice between Israel and her neighbors was punctuated by violent incidents, and there were repeated threats of the outbreak of yet another war.

Several members of the Committee had previously conducted interviews with leaders and citizens of countries involved in the conflict. We reviewed this material and decided to expand it and focus our attention on personal perceptions of involvement in past or potential wars. Each member of the Committee sought out and interviewed citizens of the involved nations. We followed an "open score" format; that is, we attempted to avoid imposing preconceptions, including

* Gregory Rochlin. MAN'S AGGRESSION: THE DEFENSE OF THE SELF (Boston: Gambit, 1973).

psychiatric ones, on the interview process and content. Some interviews were carried out in the United States; a considerable number in the Middle East during visits by Committee members. Some of the individuals whose experiences are described and whose attitudes are quoted in the report have been introduced to members of the Committee by either Palestinian or Israeli officials. The Appendix to this report describes findings from systematic interviews with a number of male Arab and Israeli graduate students carried out over two and a half years by one member. We did not seek representativeness or randomness of our sample, as our study is not of publics or governments but of individuals who identify closely with their national societies.

This method of approach involved a number of technical problems. First, although all of us are professionally involved in psychotherapeutic practice and consequently are experienced in dealing with profound human emotions and our reactions to them, we soon realized that the intensity of feeling aroused by discussion of war participation, coupled with reduction of personal restraint in discussing such subjects, provoked powerful responses in our subjects and in ourselves. We have been assailed by personal fear, doubt, anger and sensitivity and have observed ourselves tempted to retreat to the safer ground of theorizing or generalizing that would permit us to avoid the terrible specificities of the involvements of our subjects. We found that the process demanded constant vigilance and effort to be impartial with respect to the international level of conflict in order to explore and evaluate the personal involvement of our subjects.

We also experienced concern for biases in our sympathies—more than half the members were of Jewish origin—and talked this out in Committee, as well as invited participation by persons of Arab origin. The concern was heightened by awareness that almost any statement or comment about the conflict would be subject to intense scrutiny and criticism by partisans and that impartial statements, if possible at all, would not be credible to them. In fact, we submitted drafts of the report to partisans several times and were not disappointed in that expectation. We have made extensive revisions to accommodate these sensitivities and delayed publication of the study when some of the issues touched upon became the subject of heated controversy. Our purpose is to contribute to a better understanding of the psychological roots of the conflict, or at least to explore a hypothesis about such roots, and that purpose would certainly be frustrated if the study were seen as having political implications. This is one of the hazards of research on contemporary political psychology.

Some critics have asserted that psychiatrists have no business considering such problems in the first place, and disapprove of our report on both scientific and political grounds. For the moment, we can only caution ourselves and our readers about the dangers of analogizing from the behavior of individuals to the behavior of complex societies; here we are studying the former in the context of the latter. Our methods should not be interpreted as providing any basis for assessing policy alternatives beyond representing a preliminary attempt to explore the proposition that such factors are ignored only at peril. Our subjects invariably urged their own policy preferences and appear to have been actuated by them, so we have exercised considerable restraint in presenting our findings.

Finally, the context of this study requires care in protecting our sources. We have felt obliged to sacrifice much richness of detail concerning personality and life history of our subjects since progress along these lines of inquiry demands stringent attention to ethical responsibility.

In analysis of the data of interviews, the Committee considered a number of hypotheses in some depth, especially those of historical-cultural elements in the outlook of people of the several nations; we considered group and conflict and communication theories, never forgetting that conflict may involve genuine incompatibilities of interest as well as powerful currents of feeling; we considered psychological dynamics by which land, the people, the state, or the enemy are endowed with qualities of objects to be loved or hated, defended or attacked, on the basis of displacement of feelings from ancestors, parents, siblings and strangers. We consider that each of these psychological constructs has a degree of validity and may contribute to the force of conflict behavior.

As we reviewed our data, another factor insistently forced itself to our attention: the involvement of the self-esteem of individuals with national events, particularly the readiness with which dispositions toward international aggression or defense were aroused by disturbance of self-esteem or self-cohesion associated with threats to the integrity of nations. We were struck, for example, by the similarity of the reaction of Palestinians to their situation after the first Arab-Israeli War with the phenomenon of rage in individuals who have experienced personal humiliation, as well as by parallels between Israeli attitudes after the 1967 War and a stage of self development marked by grandiosity and psychological merger with idealized objects. We noted that gains in self-esteem on the part of Egyptians and other Arabs after the 1973 crossing of the Suez Canal were out of proportion to realistic military accomplishment. In short, the responses of our subjects to events that befell their nations more closely resembled the dynamic patterns of self than they reflected rational assessment or any other identifiable psychological mechanism.

Such observations led us to review patterns of war-participation of individuals in terms of the powerful dynamics of the development, defense and reactivity of the self, knowledge of which has been emerging in current development of the theory of narcissism based on psychoanalytic studies of individuals and those manifested by our subjects in relation to vicissitudes of their nations; in the latter case they often acted by political participation, including extraordinary risk-taking and aggression in their personal war involvements.

What is reported here is data drawn from individuals engaged in the conflicts and war behavior of their nations considered in relation to theory and clinical observations of the personal self. Our hypothesis is that there is an intimate linkage between personal and social-political behavior mediated by the dynamics of the self and its extensions. We hope that the theory and methods we explore may open the way for a more precise delineation of the dynamics and consequences of such personal involvement, an element that until now has seldom been included in consideration of international relationships.

Due to the fact that psychoanalytic study of individuals takes place *within* a social context, where the emotional climate and assumptions about reality are shared by analyst and subject alike, the extensions of the self to national self-objects have seldom been observed or remarked on. It is only when the observations are conducted *between* such human groups, as we have done in this study, that it becomes evident that the group or the nation is a very strongly invested self-object, that one's nationality becomes part of one's extended self.

Emergent hypothesis

Psychoanalytic study of the emergence, development, and dynamics of the individual self has delineated the mechanisms of very early self formation. The sense of self as a mental content emerges gradually in the process of separation-individuation from a state in which the infant recognizes no distinction between it and mother. Its strength is so largely shared with or, rather, borrowed from the mother that impotent frustration prompts the emergence of a spectrum of regressive and aggrandizing maneuvers, including fantasies of delusional grandiosity and omnipotence and efforts at merger with idealized parents and other powerful images. Gradual taming and modulation via appropriate responses from the parents leads to an effective sense of worth and esteem, and even fuels ambitions and ideals in favorable developmental sequences.

When the sense of self-worth, esteem, or competence is diminished by defeat, humiliation, slight, or criticism the reaction to such narcissistic injury is intense rage and aggression directed toward the perceived source of injury or threat. There may be a simultaneous regression to either an unrealistic grandiosity or merging with an idealized object. Aggression, then, is a reaction to threat or injury to self-esteem or self-coherence. The aim of such narcissistic aggression is the destruction or humiliation of the offending agent.

The psychoanalytic study of narcissistic personalities, persons whose self-absorption can be seen as an attempt to compensate for a lack of mature self-esteem, has repeatedly demonstrated that intense hostility arises out of failure to obtain gratification of the need for recognition, and this is often expressed in tyrannical and dominating behavior.

A normal mechanism for enhancing self-esteem during self-development is merger with idealized others, beginning with the earliest parenting figures. This is a process that then extends itself to the entire family, continuing throughout life, so that self-esteem is enhanced by merger of the self with this and other primary groups, which are then treated as self-objects, as extensions of the self. Ultimately, this comes to include the nation, its symbols, its territory, and its leaders. When the status or integrity or boundaries of such groups are threatened, the individual responds as though part of himself is threatened with injury or humiliation. The destructive aggression that is aroused is directed toward the perceived source of humiliation, except that in the case of group aggression this is not impeded by conscience or realistic restraints; hence, there is relatively little resistance in the individual to participation in group aggression, the most organized form of which is war. Indeed, such participation may heighten the self-esteem of individuals due to approval and recognition that is accorded within the primary group.

The role of injured narcissism in group aggression has as yet been little studied psychoanalytically due to the usual focus of such study on the personal self within the social context. It is only when individuals are approached in terms of social self-extensions that reactive dynamics of the self system become evident. This is especially true cross-nationally. In our interviews in the Middle East, we noted avid needs for national recognition, a striking tendency of individuals to identify and seek to merge with an idealized nation or its leadership, a capacity to participate in grandiose and exhibitionistic national claims, and vulnerability to despair and narcissistic rage in response to perceived national humiliation or threats. These responses parallel patterns of reaction to injury to self-cohesion or self-esteem of individuals. More positively, we noted growth of self-esteem in association with pride in the accomplishments of nations, and particularly in response to mirroring acknowledgment by others, including the adversary, phenomena also noted in the self-development of individuals. Recovery from injury to esteem of the extended national self and consequently from the impulse to war-participation appears to be just as possible in group life as it is in personal development.

Conclusions

We do not consider that our data rigorously prove our hypothesis; there are many variables and distorting factors and we have studied only a single case. But by the common-sense criterion of "inter-subjective testability," it does make sense to us and we present the material in order to provide at least a stepping-stone toward exploring what we consider a vital and little understood problem—why do people go to war?

On one matter, we wish to be emphatic. Judging from our assessment of the subjects whom we have interviewed, explanations of war-participation based on "sick" or psychopathological models are untenable. Personally healthy and broad-visioned persons participate voluntarily, efficiently, and even enthusiastically in the wars of their nations. Similarly, many of these persons had the requisite strength of character to stand against social compulsion if they disagreed with the acts of their governments. Consequently, in our judgment, theories of social compliance have limited explanatory force unless they are coupled with psychological mechanisms within the individual.

In order to maintain a focus on the hypothesis and the material from which it has emerged, we have reluctantly omitted discussion of how the theory and observations fit into the matrix of broader psycho-political theory and will only say here that it appears to us that we may have begun to explore an important psychological basis for vital linkages between the person and his society.

In the first chapter we summarize developments in understanding of the origins, elements and relevance of the theory of the self. It is written for professionals and may not be of much interest to the general reader, though we hope the other chapters will. The second chapter briefly examines some of the history and political realities of the Middle East as we have come to understand these. We are aware of pitfalls in emphasis since interpretations of history vary sharply with the vantage point of observation but we have highlighted those elements that seemed most salient to the people of the area with whom we have spoken. In Chapter 3 we report on our interviews with Palestinians; in Chapter 4, our interviews with Israelis; and in Chapter 5 we sum up our impressions. An Appendix describes a systematic exploration of geographic investments, supporting the hypothesis from a different angle of approach. We have only incidentally touched upon the outlooks of people of neighboring Arab states.

Finally, although we are not concerned here with the resolution of political or international relations issues, we believe that our data suggest a process of maturing in the qualities of self-investment in the nation on each side of the conflict, although the depth of passion involved and the significance of its impact on the behavior of the parties should not be underestimated. This apparent maturing provides some grounds for cautious optimism about the ultimate resolution of the conflict, especially as leaderships learn to reduce costly frictions that arise from inadvertent threat and hurt feelings.

1

THE CONCEPT OF SELF: EXTENDED SELF AND VICISSITUDES OF NARCISSISM

In our effort to conceptualize and clarify the psychological dimensions of conflict in the Middle East, we became convinced that the most widely accepted theories of human aggression are inadequate in their explanatory power. Those formulations which offered insight in the form of the nuclear family level of conflict and led to statements such as rape of the mother-land or devotion to the father-land seemed contrived. Formulations based on gross imitations and identifications of conflicts with early family figures or on sibling rivalries, all seemed to us sterile and insufficient as explanations that could account for the motivations and actions of the peoples of the Middle East. Rather, we felt that these formulations were guilty of the worst aspects of psychologizing. Statements about whole populations in which major nosological psychiatric categories were used, such as "the German nation is paranoid," also seemed to fall into the trap of extrapolating from individuals who were ill to nations who behaved in similar ways, but often with many more differences. Clearly, large groups have properties of the individuals that comprise them, but also the group has to be considered as more and less than the sum of its parts. There remains the conviction that national behavior cannot be thoroughly understood without consideration of individual psychology and behavior.

We speak of "individual psychology and behavior," but only of "national behavior," because the validity of the concept of a national psychology remains an open question. True, we assume it or something like it in speaking of "na-

407

tional mood" or "national will" and we try to measure it in public opinion polls, but we have trouble defining it. This is one of the many areas in which psychiatrists are puzzled as to how to integrate general theories of individual and group psychology with their general cultural and historical perspectives.

The body of this chapter will summarize recent developments in a psychoanalytic theory of the self and its extensions to national symbols and territory that holds promise of providing an explanation of the psychological linkage between the individual and society. The self structure which is a property of individuals becomes extended to incorporate primary groups such as the nation within its fabric. Thereafter, vicissitudes of the nation are experienced as happening to the self. Dynamic responses to threats to cohesiveness and reactivity to injury of self-esteem are mobilized by events befalling the nation and significantly determine decisions and behavior taken for the nation; conversely, individual self-esteem is enhanced by accomplishments of the nation.

Group narcissism originates in shared but individually incorporated mental representations of the nation that are reinforced by social validation. Mass response to critical events reflects the aggregate of common (modal) individual reactions which may be shared, manipulated or acted on by leaders.

Aggression and a specific type of rage are typical responses to injury to self-esteem that may be manifested in group behavior, including support for and participation in war and inter-group violence.

The writers are conscious that the theory of self and its implications presented here is difficult to grasp, but hope that the case examples in the following chapters will demonstrate its relevance and encourage studies toward more elegant and programmatic statements of the theory and its application.

Developmental theory of the self

In the course of our explorations, a new model of seemingly high explanatory value came to our attention. It seemed to be not only tailor-made for a description of individual psychological maturation, but also highly pertinent to group behavior as well. It involved the consideration of narcissism and the psychology of the self. While this model has a long history, we were especially impressed by the formulations of Heinz Kohut, who extended Freud's thoughts on narcissism,[1,2,3,4] considered it a separate developmental line, and reconstructed a psychology of the self which could simultaneously accommodate clinical observations of psychiatric patients and the demands of a general theory of individual depth psychology.

Webster's Dictionary offers the definition of narcissism as: "Self love; excessive interest in one's own appearance, comfort, importance, abilities, etc." In psychoanalytic psychology it is usually understood to refer to the psychological energy (libido) with which the self, as opposed to other people, is invested (cathected). The pejorative connotation of narcissism, *based on the myth of Narcissus as well as its use in* [considered it a separate developmental line, and] psychiatric terminology and some pathological developments of its outcome, should not be allowed to obscure its normal pathways, universality, and importance in human development. The biological survival of the individual requires that a great deal of psychological energy be expended on the self, physical and psychological.

The concept of the term "self" has an interesting history in psychology. George Herbert Mead described the self essentially as a social structure which arises from social experience.[5] Thus to Mead, when there is a breaking up of a complete unitary self into component selves, these aspects apply to the different social groups to which the person belongs. William James used the term "social self."

The neo-Freudians, chiefly Harry Stack Sullivan and Karen Horney, also found the term "self" central in their thinking. Sullivan stated that by the experience of rewards, parental tenderness, learning by the anxiety gradient, and approval there occurs in childhood an initial personification of experience which results in a "me" which is centrally related to the body. The three personifications are "not-me," "good-me," and "bad-me."[6] Only the latter two comprise the developing "self-dynamism" so crucial in further educative experience. The roots of the self begin in the last third of the first year of life.

Horney speaks of the "real self," which is the central inner force of all growth.[7] She gives credit to Erich Fromm for being the first to point out that the loss of the self is a central concept in understanding neurosis, although even prior to that Otto Rank described a similar notion in his concept of "Will and Creativeness."[8] She also harkens back to James's concept of the "real me." Her approach to narcissism in her book on NEUROSIS AND HUMAN GROWTH begins to approximate the theory we will be presenting here.[9]

Freud's use of the word "Ich," which may be translated as "I" but is more usually translated "ego," has essentially two meanings. It is the totality of one's own person in contrast to all other persons or objects. This is essentially the way Hartmann used it.[10] Or it may be defined as the system "ego," one of the three psychic agencies (id, ego, superego) that are now so well known to psychoanalysis, but have stimulated a great deal of dissatisfaction because they seem to be rather cold abstractions and at some distance from the direct clinical data.

When Hartmann saw the necessity for including narcissism in structural theory, he used self in contradistinction to other persons, and therefore narcissism became self-cathexis rather than ego-cathexis. Cathexis of self becomes equivalent to self-representations which may be included in ego, superego or id. This tripartite division then becomes not a competing but merely a higher level of abstractions.

Jacobson (1954) elaborated the whole concept of self-representations, and this concept has become central to much psychoanalytic thinking.[11] This is particularly true for many British psychoanalysts influenced by the writing of Sandler and Rosenblatt, who in turn were under the influence of Anna Freud. Also in Britain, Winnicott, in his work with very early developmental defects, was led to postulate a psychic organization which he called the false self, which had developed in defense of the true self, the very terms that we have seen in Horney's work on the self.[12] Lichtenstein (1964) called attention to the emergence of a primary identity, or self,[13] and his and other formulations arose out of problems in explaining the psychodynamics of borderline and psychotic persons, the very area that Freud had hoped (1914) would be the key to the further elucidation of the early concepts of narcissism that he had enunciated.[14]

Psychoanalytic theory has always recognized that the newborn, lacking adequate neurological and sensory apparatus and sensory experience, lives in a psychological state in which subject and object are not differentiated. Initially, there is no self, but only variations of tension decrease and increase. Self emerges from diverse fragments of internal self nuclei (Glover–"ego nuclei") combined with the experience of maternal response in this objectless world of primary narcissism.[15] The empathic primary caretaking person, usually the mother, makes it possible for the fleeting self experience to emerge associated with feelings of pleasure. Nonetheless, episodes of unpleasant feelings of anxiety and panic are unavoidable. This fragile self becomes an integrated whole via the caretaker's soothing and echoing responses. As this development proceeds both on its own and via interaction with the environment, it is modified and achieves coherence by the mother's emotional responses which run the spectrum of approval to disapproval, with many nuances in between. The mother's showing of her attitudes to her child has prompted the metaphor "mirroring," which at the prideful, approving end of the spectrum constitutes the "gleam in the mother's eye" that does so much for her child's self-esteem, and at the other end of the spectrum selectively responds to or even rejects certain aspects of the emerging self. Consequently, there is a continuous progressive integration and disintegration occurring under the impact of the mother's responses. Though this is difficult to pin-point chronologically, and much of this formulation is based on retrospective reconstruction from psychoanalytic treatment of adults, this process occurs early in the second year of life; the interactions of the maternal figure and the developing cohesive self apparently contribute as much to the development of the nuclear self as do biological and constitutional factors.

Kohut suggested that the nuclear self is a bipolar configuration, with one pole being the grandiose-exhibitionistic self and the other the idealized parental imago. Smooth integration of these two major constellations requires responsive participation of the parent so that grandiose fantasies can be tamed into ambitions and the idealized parental figures can serve as guiding ideals. The school-age (latency) period appears to be the time which can therefore be viewed along two dimensions: 1) *Cohesiveness* of these configurations, with a relative vulnerability or resistance to fragmentation, and 2) *Transformation* of archaic ambitions and ideals into the realizable purposes and values of life. Kohut challenged the notion that narcissism eventuated in object love. He pointed out that the U-shaped tube analogy—water going up in one side, necessitating it going down in another—as a description of narcissism as opposed to object love, made sense of some situations (such as the difficulty of being in love while one suffered from a toothache) but failed to explain others, such as the heightened sense of well-being that somebody in love feels, a far cry from the hydraulic analogy of being drained and empty. In his treatment of patients with narcissistic personality disorders, he began to see a crucial concept emerging; narcissism seemed to have a developmental line of its own and did not eventuate in object love. However, he did recognize the importance of ongoing object relationships, of which narcissistic object relationships would be a major category. From this vantage point he was able to extrapolate way stations along the line of this developmental sequence, and even describe the eventual outcome of healthy narcissistic strivings as resulting in empathy, wisdom, humor, creativity, and the acceptance of transience.

We have seen that a necessary corollary to this emphasis on narcissism is that the psychology of the self becomes a necessary and useful subordinate concept to that of the usual structural division of id, ego, and superego.

Lichtenstein was probably the first person in recent years to note that this line of theoretical formulation "contains as radical a revolution" as did Freud's introduction of structural theory in 1923.[16] It arose in part due to a pressing need on the part of analysts for a theory of object relationships. However, this required a differentiation of the "object" into two differing aggregates.

The first meaning of the term object is that used by Anna Freud in her description of the developmental line of "dependency" to "adult relationships."[17] All these object-related behaviors can be observed from an external frame of reference. A parallel set of assumptions from an intrapsychic point of view is the concept of the "representational world" as described by Sandler and Rosenblatt (1962).[18] With Jacobson (1964) they describe the lengthy process of the developmental line of a set of mental representations of the child's own self (self-representations), and of the various persons with whom the child has significant interactions over the years (object-representations). The idiosyncratic nature of both of these processes of internalization make the individual prone to distortions, both of the self and the other, and therefore of his perception of external reality.

Once we have made the distinction between object relations and object love, we can reexamine the concept of objects supplying functions to the immature psyche which will be experienced as parts of the self. In terms of the libido theory, these objects become need-fulfilling and invested with narcissistic libido. Kohut has proposed that these be called *self-objects*. The relation of the child with these archaic objects is not part of the developmental sequence of object love. They are wholly within the line of development of narcissism. We must remember that the development of object love can only begin after the secure differentiation of the self from the object.

Kohut has stressed that these objects are not loved for their attributes, even though there may be cognitive differentiation of such attributes. Modell (1968) calls these transitional objects, which the child creates in order to control the actual mother, who is no longer under his control but has her own center of volition.[19]

Basic to this theory of an independent line of development of the self has been the clinical importance of the sense of cohesion and transformation of self. Although we have seen that both Hartmann and Jacobson preferred to use the self as a non-psychological construct, Kohut has suggested that organized systems of memories (self-representations) have both a dynamic and genetic significance. They therefore can be elevated to the status of a personality reality, and in their organized form can be called "the self."

The most recent complete summary of psychoanalytic theory by Gedo and Goldberg (1973) expresses a clear preference for this term over the term identity, with which it has much in common.[20] Erikson used the term identity at one time to describe a conscious sense of individual identity, at another to describe an unconscious striving from continuity or cohesiveness of personal character, at still other times as a criterion for the silent doings of ego synthesis, and finally, as a maintenance of an inner solidarity with a group's ideals and identity.[21] We have seen that other writers have also recognized the importance of self, such as the self-concept of George Herbert Mead and William James, the self-system of Harry Stack Sullivan, and the fluctuating self-experiences described by Federn and Schilder. Greenacre used the term self-images, which are vitalized by constant comparison and contrast with others.[22] Mahler suggested that self-differentiation occurred in the 18th month period in relation to separation-individuation from the object, and suggested that from about age three to age six a stable integration of self-identity occurred.[23] Eissler reasoned that the experience of self-cognizance, "I am," deserved to be labeled a fourth structure of the mind, and emerged at puberty to serve the function of self and a sense of personal identity. Lichtenstein summarized all these by saying that there was a self which comprised the total potential range of all possible variations of the individual's identity which are compatible with his "identity theme."

The concept of identity has often been, and still is used synonymously with the concept of self, and at the level of personal and group interaction the concept of identity remains a useful operational bridge.

Kohut, however, sees the self as a depth-psychological concept and referring to the core of the personality makeup of the child's interplay with his earliest self-objects. It contains a person's basic ambitions, his most central idealized goals, the basic talent and skills that mediate between ambitions and goals—all that attached to the sense of being a unit in time and space, a recipient of impressions, and an initiator of actions. Identity, on the other hand, is the point of convergence between the striving of the *developed* self (as it is constituted in late adolescence and early adulthood) and the socio-cultural position of the individual.

Kohut maintains that this differentiation is very fruitful. Some individuals are, for example, characterized by a strong, firm, well-defined self that was acquired early in life—but their identity is, due to later circumstances, quite diffuse. The personality of certain types of physicians belongs to such a pattern. The diffuseness of their identity permits empathy with many different types of people—yet the firm self protects against fragmentation. There are other people whose organization is the very opposite: a weak self, but a strong, perhaps overly strong and rigid identity. These are individuals whose cohesion is maintained by an intensely experienced social role, an intensely experienced ethnic or religious sense of belonging, etc. And these are people who, when their identity is taken from them (e.g., when they move from one culture to another), will disintegrate. And there are, finally, still others whose firm but not rigid identity rests on a firmly established self.

Identity, or the personal sense of being an individual different from others (a coherent self, therefore) and yet continuously the same, derives not only from genetically determined characteristics such as morphology and constitution, but from the psychological incorporation of attributes from significant people in the immediate environment (identification). Whereas in the pre-school years this means one's parents, the process extends in time to include the extended family, the peer group, social reference groups, and "culture heroes" in various realms of activity.

The concept of the extended self

These processes of identification which are so crucial in leading to a final, cohesive sense of identity have been well described by Erikson, and have been seminal for the study of psychohistory which has arisen from his work.[24] What we are hypothesizing in this study is that there is an even earlier process which precedes the consolidation of identity, which we have pointed out requires a whole and integrated self. We are suggesting that the concept of self-objects, which are necessary for the psychological survival of the developing self, are even more fundamental for understanding the un-remitting rage and thirst for revenge of the proportions that have been encountered among the people involved in the Middle East conflict, and of similar conflicts elsewhere. These self-objects are included in what we are calling the *extended self*. Thus the flag, the earth, the hills and trees, much of the inanimate world in which one grows up take on the attributes of self-objects, since they seem to serve a basic function of psychic regulation, much as did the mother in the early phases of the development of self. To lose these is to risk the fragmentation of self, an eventuality which people will resist with their very lives. John F. Kennedy may have recognized the basic human need to identify on the deep level with one's city or country when he proclaimed from the Brandenburg Gate: *"Ich bin ein Berliner!"* Self is more important than life; the terrorist movement in the Middle East attests to the grim truth of this assertion.

There appears to be almost a biologically based need on man's part to attach himself during his growth years to the family and its extensions, not only because of survival con-siderations, but also through the operation of needs which express themselves in play. This play among the young is deeply rooted and can be observed in many other animal species. It has a vital role in the socialization of the human and involves his adoption of some group identity. Cultures universally formalize and facilitate the phenomenon of play and incorporate it in the process of enculturation. The en-culturative process thus leads to group loyalties, such as to team, school, religion and nation.

The first scene of fluctuant interaction of the individual and group identity is in the family, where the step from "my identity" to "our identity" is as easy as the change from "my family" to "our family," which, like the mother who makes the latter phrase plural, is in fact felt to be an extension of the self, a self-object.

During puberty and adolescence, an idealization comes to occupy a dominant place in mental life; identification with culture heroes extends to contemporary and historical figures of national significance, to sports stars or movie stars, to legendary and literary heroes, and others, progressively incorporating their attributes into a consolidated sense of personal identity. Language, and especially rhetoric, are laden with the relics of this process; motherland, fatherland, brothers-in-arms, etc., now become not merely glib metaphors, but express the conscious residues of psychologically significant, group-shared perceptions of correspondence between entities of different orders.

Many authors have sought a concept of self and identity which could function as a bridge between individual and group psychology. Whereas Erikson recognized the social psychological use of the term identity, it remained for Kohut in the psychoanalytic treatment of patients with narcissistic personality disorders to differentiate the concept of self as an intrapsychic depth concept which manifests itself in later interpersonal relations, and particularly in the transference relationship with the analyst.

The two types of narcissistic transference constellations Kohut described may be extrapolated to intra and intergroup relations. To recapitulate, in the first type, the mirror transferences, there is an emergence of an archaic grandiose self with exaggerated fantasies of perfection, beauty, omnipotence, and omniscience. This archaic self mirrors itself in the analyst's presence; and in an even more archaic form, the analyst is experienced as an alter-ego, or twin, who is exactly like the patient. In the most regressive subtype of the mirror transference, the patient feels merged with the analyst, who becomes a continuity of the grandiose self. The other main type of narcissistic transferences have been called the idealized transferences. The analyst is admired as being endowed with unlimited knowledge and power, or at least as a magnificent and awe-inspiring person. Genetically, the child has tried to preserve his original perfection by assigning it to an idealized parental imago, an omnipotent object.

These processes are active, not only developmentally and in the psychoanalytic treatment setting, but in daily relations with others close to us, with national leaders, the national group, and with other nations. They constitute a powerful, unconscious force which commands and shapes the development of certain national movements and positions. An inherent attribute of these processes is their impetus to the emergence of leaders. Certain members of a society, as part of their charismatic and psycho-political skills, discern more clearly the group aspiration; they identify with it and come to personify the group self and ethos. In turn, the most outstanding leaders may even shape the nation to a degree. There is a conundrum of considerable importance to politics with which Tolstoy concerned himself; that is, does man emerge to lead the nation in a particular direction or does the direction of the nation find a man to lead it? The question is, of course, artificial, since to some extent the process is circular. A man such as Churchill, thoroughly saturated with his English identity, came to personify his country, and so inspired sufficient numbers of his countrymen to move in a particular direction that Britain may be said to have taken on some of the attributes of the man.*

The context of national mood or need to a large extent

---

* It is interesting to note that while the man may go on playing the part of his nation, the larger unit may paradoxically change direction more quickly, and leave an erstwhile great leader looking anachronistic.

determines the types of leaders which may arise, particularly in groups which are threatened with loss of group cohesion, similar to the loss of the cohesive self in individual psychology. Groups seem to resist fragmentation with an equal strength to that of the individual. The omnipotent leader is either a savior as an idealized object (the Moshe Dayan of 1967–73) or disappoints in his failure to exert magical powers (the discredited Dayan following the October 1973 War); or such leaders may emerge as a consequence of their own grandiose personalities in conjunction with the moment of national need for heroic leadership (the Churchill of World War II); or leaders may be assigned such perfection and power by a yearning nation (Eisenhower of the Normandy landing). In mature development, narcissism becomes modulated and even transformed into such character assets as empathy, creativeness, humor, wisdom, and a related acceptance of a sense of human and personal transience and ambiguity. This transformation, however, is seldom complete, and we find that there are foci of unmodified and archaic narcissism, which in the face of frustration manifest themselves in poorly controlled, impotent rage and destructive omnipotence.

Among current psychoanalysts, Rochlin and Fromm in particular have recognized the importance of narcissism in the stimulation of aggression. Rochlin particularly points out that man's aggression is in defense of self, and he even changes the usual question as to what makes man so aggressive and hateful into what makes man so prone to humiliation and vulnerable to injury.[25] He suggests that narcissistic humiliation, plus the license that goes with group sanction, combines into a dangerous amalgam. Fromm points out that this "group narcissism," which involves unforgiving injury—when, for example, one's country is slighted—is so easily labeled and rationalized as patriotism and loyalty that the vengeful person's motives are never questioned.[26]

Otto Kernberg's observations of rageful aggression in the treatment relationships of individuals suffering from pathological narcissism closely parallel those of Kohut descriptively; especially, he notes a propensity for a sudden breakdown of surface adaptation in response to disappointments from the analyst and destructive attacks on the whole relationship.[27] Kernberg differs from Kohut's theoretical views at several points, especially with respect to the origins of pathologic narcissism in disturbed early object relationships. While we consider that technical and theoretical differences are necessary and fruitful in refining a new level of understanding, these differences do not significantly affect the basis for our hypothesis that injury of self-regard is a principal source of group aggression. We have not attempted to reconcile or integrate these differences here as this is a concern for personality theorists. Rather, we have chosen to base our discussion on Kohut's developmental theory since pathological models are inappropriate to the study of universally shared group phenomena, although it is illuminating to observe the similarity of dynamics between pathological behavior in the individual and group reaction that would be considered normal under certain social circumstances.

What characterizes narcissistic rage in the spectrum of human aggressive responses is that it expresses the need to right a wrong and undo a hurt. It results in an unrelenting compulsion in the pursuit of this vengeful "justice," which gives no surcease to those who have suffered a narcissistic injury. And narcissistic injury may vary in intensity from subtle depreciation, to ridicule, to conspicuous defeat.

Kohut points out that the enemy who elicits this archaic rage is seldom understood by the narcissistically vulnerable. There is a suspension of empathy and rational analysis, so that the enemy "is seen by him not as an autonomous source of impulsions, but as a flaw in a narcissistically perceived reality."[28] (This is a clear mechanism for the dehumanization of the enemy we have so often seen.) The enemy represents a

422 Self-Involvement in Middle East Conflict

recalcitrant part of an expanded self over which the individual expects to exercise full control and whose mere independence or otherness is an offense.

Narcissistic rage arises when the self-object fails to live up
to the absolutist expectations. While this occurs in all individuals, the most violent forms of narcissistic rage arise in
those persons for whom a sense of absolute control over an
archaic environment is indispensable, because the maintenance of self-esteem and of coherence of the self depends on
the unconditional availability of the approving mirroring
functions of an admiring self-object or on the ever present
opportunity for a merger with an idealized one.

At the group or national level these feelings lead to an
expression of narcissistic rage in which the self, the extensions of the self, or the extended self are seen as being
violated. In this regard the self extends to incorporate one's
home, land, village, local customs, etc. Group cohesion,
Kohut points out, is maintained by not only a shared ego-
ideal, but also a shared grandiose self. Or, stated in another
way, groups are held together as much by their ambitions as
their aims. Groups may also, like individuals, show re-
gressions when there is blocking of grandiose ambitions or
shared ideals. They then resort to group aggression, which in
its relentless search for revenge has all the attributes of
chronic narcissistic rage, and when engaged in by a nation
takes on the dimensions of war.

What this new approach to the psychology of the self
offers is that there is a much more archaic relation with the
self-objects of family, local community, country, and homeland than an object love orientation would have led us to
consider. The survivor orientation described by Robert J.
Lifton in his recent works suggests that those self-objects
intensify the survivor's orientation to his homeland, since in
early phases of development such self-objects were necessary
for the very survival of the self.[29]

We are, therefore, led to conclude that a deeper rather

MENTAL HEALTH MATERIALS CENTER

PUBLICATIONS OFFICE
30 East 29th Street
New York NY 10016
[212] 889-5760

GAP PUBLICATIONS LIST AND ORDER FORM

All Group for the Advancement of Psychiatry titles currently in print are included in this list. Out-of-print publications are contained in the bound volumes described on page 4.

To place your order, please check below the titles you want, complete the form on page 4, and mail as directed. ALL PRICES ARE SUBJECT TO CHANGE WITHOUT NOTICE.

CODE NO.	TITLE & DATE OF PUBLICATION	NO. OF COPIES	UNIT PRICE	AMOUNT
	ADOLESCENCE			
1-68	Normal Adolescence: Its Dynamics and Impact—2/68 .		$ 4.00	
1-101	Power and Authority in Adolescence: The Origins and Resolutions of Intergenerational Conflict—5/78 .		6.50	
	AGING			
2-12	The Right to Die: Decision and Decision Makers (Symposium)—11/77 .		4.00	
1-81	The Aged and Community Mental Health: A Guide to Program Development—11/71 .		4.00	
1-79	Toward a Public Policy on Mental Health Care of the Elderly—11/70 .		2.00	
1-59	Psychiatry and the Aged: An Introductory Approach—9/65 .		2.00	
	CHILD PSYCHIATRY			
1-87	From Diagnosis to Treatment: An Approach to Treatment Planning for the Emotionally Disturbed Child—8/73 .		4.50	
1-111	The Process of Child Psychiatry - 10/82 .		12.50	
1-62	Psychopathological Disorders in Childhood: Theoretical Considerations and a Proposed Classification—6/66 .		6.50	
1-38	The Diagnostic Process in Child Psychiatry—8/57 .		2.00	
	COLLEGE STUDENT			
1-92	The Educated Woman: Prospects and Problems—1/75 .		4.00	
1-60	Sex and the College Student—11/65 .		2.00	
1-52	The College Experience: A Focus for Psychiatric Research—5/62 .		2.00	
	COMMUNITY			
1-102	The Chronic Mental Patient in the Community—5/78 .		4.00	
1-94	The Psychiatrist and Public Welfare Agencies—11/75 .		3.00	
1-85	The Welfare System and Mental Health—7/73 .		2.00	
	FAMILY			
1-78	The Field of Family Therapy—3/70 .		4.00	
1-76	The Case History Method in the Study of Family Process—3/70 .		5.00	
1-106	Divorce, Child Custody and the Family—9/80 .		12.95	

ORDERING INFORMATION

Please indicate on pages 1-3 the titles you wish to order. Complete the Order Form including subscription information if necessary. Mail the completed form with your remittance as specified to the Publications Office. Orders not accompanied by agency, institution, or organization purchase order must be accompanied by remittance.

This publication list supersedes all other lists. All prices are subject to change without notice.

ORDER FORM

Mental Health Materials Center
30 East 29th Street
New York NY 10016   [212] 889-5760

1. Please enter total amount of order as noted at bottom of previous page............. $ _____

2. Add postage & handling charges as follows:
   Orders less than $10, add $1
   Orders more than $10 but less than $50, add 10% of total order............. _____
   Orders more than $50 but less than $100, add 8% of total order............. _____

3. Subscription to Vol 11 series of GAP Publications:
   [ ] $48 domestic............. _____
   [ ] $55 foreign............. _____

   Total order $ _____

[ ] check enclosed
[ ] please bill

Name _____ [please print]

Agency _____

Street _____

City _____ State _____ Zip _____

QUANTITY DISCOUNTS ON SINGLE TITLES

1- 9 copies......... @ list price
10- 24 copies......... @ list less 15%
25- 99 copies......... @ list less 20%
100-499 copies......... @ list less 30%
500 or more copies...... quotation upon request

SUBSCRIPTION INFORMATION

GAP publications may be ordered by subscription. They are issued on an irregular schedule in a volume series that covers a 3-year period. During any particular subscription series, about 1,000 pages of text are customarily issued. (About 7-10 publications) Subscriptions must be entered on the basis of a complete volume series, covering the designated 3-year period. No exceptions can be made to this arrangement.

The current subscription cycle comprises the Vol 11 series issued during the 3-year period July 1, 1980-June 30, 1983. Subscription orders received during this period commence with Publication #107. Cost of subscription is $48 in USA, and $55 in Canada and other foreign countries—payable in US currency. On receipt of your Vol 11 subscription, we will send you all publications issued to date in this series.

GAP PUBLICATIONS CATALOG

On request, a descriptive catalog of GAP Publications is available. It describes the contents of many titles listed in this announcement. It also lists all titles contained in each clothbound book for Vols 1-10 (see page 3), including publications otherwise unobtainable because they are of print.

than more superficial understanding of the individual's investment in intense intergroup or national conflict is necessary for the understanding of the implacability of the mutual positions taken by the antagonists, such as those caught up in the turmoil and agony of the Middle East conflict.

References

1. H. Kohut. Forms and Transformations of Narcissism. *Journal of the American Psychoanalytic Association* 14 (1966) 243–272.
2. ———. "The Psychoanalytic Treatment of Narcissistic Personality Disorders," in THE PSYCHOANALYTIC STUDY OF THE CHILD Vol. 23 (New York: International Universities Press, 1968), pp 86–113.
3. ———. THE ANALYSIS OF THE SELF (New York: International Universities Press, 1971).
4. ———. "Thoughts on Narcissism and Narcissistic Rage," in THE PSYCHOANALYTIC STUDY OF THE CHILD Vol. 27 (New York: Quadrangle Books, 1972), pp 360–400.
5. G. H. Mead. MIND, SELF AND SOCIETY (Chicago: University of Chicago Press, 1934).
6. H. S. Sullivan. CONTRIBUTIONS OF HARRY STACK SULLIVAN. P. Mullany, ed. (New York: Hermitage House, 1952).
7. Karen Horney. NEW WAYS IN PSYCHOANALYSIS (New York: W. W. Norton, Inc., 1939).
8. O. Rank. WILL THERAPY (New York: Alfred A. Knopf, 1936).
9. Karen Horney. NEUROSIS AND HUMAN GROWTH (New York: W. W. Norton, Inc., 1950).
10. H. Hartmann. "Comments on the Psychoanalytic Theory of the Ego," in ESSAYS IN EGO PSYCHOLOGY (New York: International Universities Press, 1950), pp 113–141.
11. E. Jacobson. THE SELF AND THE OBJECT WORLD (New York: International Universities Press, 1964).
12. See citation 7.
13. H. Lichtenstein. The Role of Narcissism in the Emergence and Maintenance of Primary Identity, *International Journal of Psychoanalysis* 45 (1964) 49–56.

14. S. Freud. ON NARCISSISM: AN INTRODUCTION (Standard Edition), Vol. 14 (London: Hogarth, 1957) pp 73–102.

15. E. Glover. THE BIRTH OF THE EGO (New York: International Universities Press, 1968).

16. H. Lichtenstein. Identity and Sexuality, *Journal of the American Psychoanalytic Association* (1961) 179–260.

17. A. Freud. NORMALITY AND PATHOLOGY IN CHILDHOOD (New York: International Universities Press, 1965).

18. J. Sandler and B. Rosenblatt. "The Concept of the Representational World," in THE PSYCHOANALYTIC STUDY OF THE CHILD, Vol. 17 (New York: International Universities Press, 1962), pp 128–148.

19. A. Modell. OBJECT LOVE AND REALITY (New York: International Universities Press, 1968).

20. J. Gedo and A. Goldberg. MODELS OF THE MIND (Chicago: University of Chicago Press, 1973).

21. E. Erikson. IDENTITY AND THE LIFE CYCLE, Psychological Issues Monograph I (New York: International Universities Press, 1959).

22. P. Greenacre. "The Influence of Infantile Trauma on Genetic Patterns," in EMOTIONAL GROWTH (New York: International Universities Press, 1967).

23. M. Mahler. "Thoughts About Development and Individuation," in THE PSYCHOANALYTIC STUDY OF THE CHILD, Vol. 18 (New York: International Universities Press, 1963), pp 307–324.

24. E. Erikson. YOUNG MAN LUTHER: A STUDY IN PSYCHOANALYSIS AND HISTORY (New York: W. W. Norton, 1958).

25. G. Rochlin. MAN'S AGGRESSION: THE DEFENSE OF THE SELF (Boston: Gambit, 1973).

26. E. Fromm. THE ANATOMY OF HUMAN DESTRUCTIVENESS (New York: Holt, Rinehart & Winston, 1972).

27. O. Kernberg. BORDERLINE CONDITIONS AND PATHOLOGICAL NARCISSISM (New York: Jason Aronson, 1975).

28. See citation 4.

29. R. J. Lifton. THOUGHT REFORM AND THE PSYCHOLOGY OF TOTALISM (New York: W. W. Norton, 1963).

2

THE POLITICAL CONTEXT

National statehood is a relatively recent form of political organization which grew out of European history and which has spread to include virtually all the peoples and to occupy all of the land surfaces of the globe—although there is still a great deal of re-defining of peoples and territories in process. There are still peoples who aspire to nationhood, nations which aspire to statehood, and states which have not achieved national mobilization of their populations. Much contemporary international strife, including the conflict in the Middle East, arises from the persistent efforts of peoples to achieve nationhood and then to establish, define, and secure the boundaries and apparatus of national statehood.

It is beyond the scope of this summary to review the historical development and differentiation of the concepts of nationalism and the thrust toward national statehood, but some essential distinctions may be made. A *people* has been defined as a group of persons who share complementary habits and facilities of communication and a common culture, and who recognize their kinship and community of purpose. As we shall see, such was the historic status of the Jewish people before the rise of Zionism, and of the Palestine Arab people before they aspired to nationhood (approximately 1917–1954).*

* This report and GAP make no judgment as to whether, or to what degree, any stage of political development or organization characterizes Palestinian people; that question has juridical and political implications and is beyond our competence. We have, however, reported on the beliefs and sentiments of our subjects with respect to the status of their community.

A *nation* is a people who have developed the organizational capability of "forming, supporting and enforcing a common will," in the words of Karl Deutsch; that is, a degree of social governance.[1] Even more distinctive, in our opinion, is the capacity of the nation to attract the highest political loyalty of its members, to become invested with sentiments of nationalism.

The ideology of self-determination and autonomy and a valued sense of distinctiveness and cultural superiority in comparison with other nations permits the psychological investment of self; the nationalist sentiment grows from a sense of the nation as an extension of self. Conversely, the social self is experienced as representative, an embodiment of the nation, as is experienced by every foreign traveler.

Finally, a *state* is a political and legal structure in which an autonomous government exercises authority over a population inhabiting a defined territory, a condition of political sovereignty. Colonies are not states, of course, as their administrations or colonial governments do not possess sovereignty.

States may evolve from nations, and indeed, a prime purpose of national movements is the achievement of statehood; but states may also precede and perhaps never achieve national mobilization within a structure of governance. Indeed, a number of contemporary states encompass several distinctive peoples and are threatened by efforts at secession and the possibility of civil war. Finally, a people may develop a sense of nationhood whether or not they can or ever will be able to form a national state.

The *national-state* is a product of the psychological and social qualities of the nation combined with the territorial, political, and governmental qualities of the state. It should be noted here that while states possess juridical qualities of sovereignty in international law and hence can claim recognition from other states, the potency of the state in international relations depends in good part on the degree of loyalty and allegiance of its population and on its support for the policies of the state. When state and nation are coterminous in a national-state structure, the mobilization of human and material resources for international purposes is powerfully enhanced; hence, the nationalism of a population exerts a strong political force in international affairs.

From the perspective of the evolving international system, the Middle East presents a kaleidoscopic pattern, with outside powers seeking to play local powers against one another, and with local powers seeking to extract advantage from their position at the least cost to themselves.

The ancient history of the Middle East as the cradle of civilization and as the starting point of three world religions has continued to exercise influence into the present. Historical myths of the memories of peoples are vividly present in modern Egypt; Israel was founded in large part on the basis of memories and historic claims some thousands of years old; the holy sites of three religions in Jerusalem affect the political sentiments of Jews, Moslems, and Christians; memories of the Islamic Caliphate have been revived in the politics of pan-Arabism. The region was a critical and exposed flank of the Ottoman Empire, a land bridge to Egypt and Africa, and the portal of entry to the hinterlands. As a consequence, an area with no great resource or independent force of its own had been continually subjected to dominance by external powers.

For twelve centuries, from the seventh century onward, different parts of the Middle East were dominated by successive Moslem empires; among them the Umayyads, Abbasids, Fatamids and Mamluks, followed in the twelfth century by the Seljuks and in the fourteenth by the Ottomans, a domination which was eroded during the eighteenth and nineteenth centuries by internal decay and European penetration and finally ended with the First World War. During these centuries a great civilization rose, experienced a golden age of eminence in science, commerce, the arts and public administration, and then gradually declined, as much from internal rigidity and corruption as from external pressures.

Until the rise of Zionism, and with it, the emergence of a sense of Jewish nationalism, Jews dispersed throughout the world were content to remember Jerusalem while a small community of the religious lived there peacefully under foreign tolerance. Until the rise of an Arab sense of nationalism, the Palestine people, whether Christian or Moslem, submitted to the changing overlordships.

European penetration of the Middle East was a tortuous process, conducted less by conquest than by an array of arrangements with local ruling groups: treaties, alliances, protectorates, mandates, commercial agreements, financial arrangements and the like. When Napoleon invaded Egypt in 1798, the target was the route to trade and influence in India and the British naval response that forced his withdrawal was in defense of those interests. Both were intent on filling the power vacuum left by the decline of Ottoman authority, but for the most part military clashes were modest in scope while the preferred method was that of aiding local parties that arose to seize fragments of declining Ottoman authority. This pattern of European jockeying for advantage through intrigue with local leaders continued through the nineteenth century and more or less faithfully reflected the shifting alliance patterns among European powers. When Russia threatened to become a dominant power beyond the Black Sea at the expense of the Ottoman Empire, Great Britain and France combined against her; when the French protege Muhammad Ali occupied Syria, Britain, Russia, Austria, and Prussia joined in an ultimatum that forced his withdrawal.

During this century of rapid transition the people, or at least the elites, of the Middle East were increasingly exposed to European thought and institutions. As Tsarist Russia pressed toward the Bosphorus from the North during the 19th century, the Ottoman rulers turned first to Prussia and after 1870 to Britain as a lesser evil and military contact became extensive. When France found herself barred by the British Navy from direct incursions, she could provide education and culture, military advisors and engineers to the quasi-independent rulers of Egypt, ultimately gaining from one of them a concession to construct the Suez Canal, only to have the British government buy out the Egyptian minority shares from a bankrupt successor. Thus European bankers and commercial interests gained increasing influence; only they could bail out one ruler after another. After the defeat of France in the Franco-German War in 1870, Germany, too, made considerable penetration through Turkey, largely by building railroads and by undertaking military training and armament sales, a foothold that laid a basis for the German-Ottoman Alliance of the First World War.

Meanwhile, the whole and various congeries of ideas that had evolved in Europe and found their expression in the American and French revolutions filtered into the consciousness of inhabitants of the area, carried to a considerable extent by imperial agents and commercial representatives, by French and American missionaries who founded schools, and by the sons of the cultured and privileged elites who were educated in the universities of Europe and of the United States. Given the centuries-long history of a number of Moslem empires and then of Ottoman rule, followed by the coercive features of European imperialism, the idea of a nation and state based on popular consent and supported by the enthusiastic devotion of its people was as novel as it was revolutionary and was resisted by every instrument of administration of the dying empire, the local suzerains and, much less consciously and effectively, by the new imperialists. Secret societies were formed and nationalist demands were issued. Political parties spread sentiments of emancipation before they were suppressed. A typical expression of nationalist sentiments was voiced by the Egyptian intellectual Mustapha Kamil, who wrote in 1896 ". . . that no sentiment is more beautiful than the love of our country, that the soul is noble, and a people without independence is a people without existence. Patriotism (nationalism) speedily raises backward peoples to civilization, greatness and power."[2] Literally hundreds of similar statements were published by Syrian, Lebanese, Iraqi, and other proponents of the Arab National Movement in the last half of the nineteenth century, even as similarly inspired visions of a new nation were being articulated by Zionist Jews and rebellious young Turks. Such utterances were perceived as a threat by the Ottoman Empire, which, after the "Young Turk" revolt of 1908, attempted to impose the Turkish language and culture upon Arab countries. Attalah Mansour claims that Arab nationalism was "a response to the attempt to impose Turkish culture on the Middle East."[3]

Political documents of Europe were translated and disseminated; by the beginning of the 20th century demonstrations and local revolts began to occur in Egypt, which was dominated by Great Britain, and in the Arabian Peninsula, still marginally under Turkish rule. The sense of nationalism, although still underground, was a growing force, sufficiently powerful to tempt Britain to use the Arab nationalists and to aid them in revolt against Turkey with the outbreak of the Great War of 1914.

While on the one hand the British fanned Arab hopes for freedom in the Hijaz, Syria and Palestine, on the other they encouraged the hopes of international Jewry for establishing a Jewish homeland in the very same territory. The idea had been favored in England by Christian Zionists since the 14th century and gained force during the 19th from the violent persecution of Eastern European Jews. Though initially they met resistance, Jewish writers and intellectuals, most notably the journalist Theodor Herzl, provided shape and substance to the idea so that it became possible to organize a World Zionist Congress in 1897 and to evolve a form of governance for a national movement. After 1906 the Zionist organization worked toward the establishment of a Jewish state in Palestine.

Before the First World War the Zionist Organization negotiated concessions from the Ottomans and purchased title to tracts of land from absentee owners; there small colonies of refugees from the pogroms of East Europe were settled—the Jewish population of Palestine rose from fewer than 40,000 at the turn of the century to about 60,000 by the end of the First World War. Meanwhile, the Hebrew language was revised and modernized—a significant symbol of the movement toward national identity.

During the war a Zionist political committee persuaded the British government to make a statement concerning Zionist interests in Palestine. The Balfour Declaration of 1917 viewed ". . . with favour the establishment in Palestine of a national home for the Jewish people . . . it being clearly understood that nothing shall be done which may prejudice the civil and religious rights of existing non-Jewish communities in Palestine . . ."

This was the third of Britain's three separate and incompatible agreements, each designed to further war aims and post-war expectations, and each based on the anticipation of dismemberment of the Turkish Empire. These famous engagements held the seeds of later conflict, as they provided a psychological and juridical base for later claims. In 1915–16 Sir Henry McMahon, speaking for the British Government, corresponded with Husain, the Sharif of Mecca, holding out promises of an independent Arab kingdom; the Arabs understood it would include Palestine.

Meanwhile, the secret Sykes-Picot Agreement between

Britain and France, entered into with the approval of Tsarist Russia, was concluded in 1916. The agreement defined post-war spheres of influence in the region, ultimately mandating Palestine, Transjordan, and Iraq to Britain. Tsarist Russia expected to gain substantial control of the Straits, a hope frustrated by the surprising revival of Turkey under Ataturk, as well as by the Soviet renunciation of Tsarist objectives. In any event, the ending of the war found Britain and France dominant in the Eastern Mediterranean, a condition soon to be legalized in the Mandate system of the League of Nations. But the "promises" were not forgotten, at least by their recipients. At the post-war conferences Zionists and Arab leaders pressed their conflicting claims in Palestine, the Zionists favoring a Mandate within which immigration could proceed, while Amir Faysal pressed for full independence within a Syrian state. The powers chose the mandatory system, with Palestine coming under British control. (Parenthetically, a Zionist Commission led by Dr. Chaim Weizmann met with Palestinian notables and Amir Faysal in 1918 to work out understandings; Weizmann and Faysal actually signed an agreement in January 1919, recognizing Jewish rights in Palestine in the event that an independent Arab Kingdom was established.) Though immigration was restricted throughout the mandatory period, by the beginning of the Second World War nearly a half-million Jews resided in Palestine. The Zionist movement had become increasingly organized and acquired all of the characteristics of an unrecognized government, including illegal but effective military forces, as well as educational and cultural institutions and international political representation: the characteristics of a nation, although not a state. Similar developments took place in the Arab community of Palestine at a somewhat slower and more uncertain rate; a political culture derived from centuries of occupation was not easily adapted to the organizational requirements of new nationhood.

Between the two World Wars the subjugation of the Middle East to Britain and France appeared quite complete, and brought with it all the apparatus of Western governance: civil administration, education, public works, commercial development. And throughout this period the Mandate powers tutored and negotiated with indigenous leaders under a variety of arrangements from the nominal independence of the Egyptian protectorate to the Governorship of Palestine. However, the deeper the penetration of European culture and administration, the greater was the spread of European ideas of nation, including the Wilsonian articulation of self-determination. In order to govern, the European powers made step by step concessions so that actual governance passed gradually into the hands of local rulers.

In a direct sense, the Second World War spilled over but slightly from Europe into the Middle East. German geopolitical theory had identified the area as important and there were some German efforts to penetrate the area, militarily in the form of Rommel's sweep of North Africa and politically by intrigues in Iraq and Egypt—involving, incidentally, a group of extreme Palestinian nationalists under the leadership of the former Grand Mufti of Jerusalem. However, German resources were so fully occupied elsewhere that little was accomplished directly. The indirect consequences were massive.

The Nazi regime in Germany, with its policies of Jewish extermination, created irresistible pressure and argument for a national refuge; the Holocaust created a large body of refugees; it bore heavily on the conscience of the West; it permanently marked the consciousness of World Jewry and virtually eliminated resistance to Zionist aspirations among both Jews and the post-war powers, including, at first, the Soviet Union. During the war and immediately afterward, the flow of Jewish immigration to Palestine, permitted and sometimes illegal, could not be contained by the mandatory power or successfully resisted by the Arab inhabitants, nor could international support for a solution which would accommodate Zionist aspirations be denied.

During the war the French and British authorities enlisted the cooperation of governments under their tutelage, but always at some price in autonomy or assurance of post-war independence; the war simply hastened dissolution of imperial processes. When the war ended, the former European imperial powers were so weakened that, even if they had wished, they could not re-establish their authority and, one by one, recognized their former dependencies as sovereign states. At the outset of the war only Turkey, Saudi Arabia, and Yemen were fully sovereign; Iraq, Iran, Egypt and Jordan were independent but subject to significant state servitudes; Syria and Lebanon were under French governors until the Free French granted nominal independence in 1941; Palestine had the status of a Crown Colony. And, although the war swirled over North Africa, the peoples and governments of the Middle East largely sat it out; despite some temptation they kept to the role of cautious neutrals. A Jewish military brigade was mobilized by the British and its members acquired military skills. Between the war's end and 1962, the number of independent states in the Middle East and North Africa had increased from five to eighteen, each state passing through the political struggles of new nationhood. Meanwhile, cold war politics entered the area.

The power vacuum created by the collapse of European imperialism and not immediately filled by the new and uncertain nations of the area almost invited Soviet encroachment, especially in view of the traditional, though intermittent, Russian interest in the Straits and the Persian Gulf. The Soviets established a short-lived puppet republic in Azerbaijan in 1946; strong diplomatic pressure and military threats were exerted on Turkey and Soviet-encouraged guerrilla forces controlled much of Greece. This alarming penetration, together with British and French inability to respond, stimulated in 1947 the enunciation of the Truman Doctrine by the United States, and massive aid to the beleaguered nations. The United States had become a participant in Middle East politics.

Access to Middle Eastern oil was in considerable part responsible for the United States's sudden and precipitate involvement in the Middle East; both Presidents Roosevelt and Truman regarded this as a "vital security interest" and much of the vigor of American willingness to fill the post-war power vacuum, especially in Iran, derived from this perception. The prize was even greater than expected as oil consumption rose from 2.4 to 6.3 million barrels a day between 1950 and 1973; parallel increases held for Europe, the Commonwealth and Japan.

Meanwhile, oil producing countries which at first had been gratified by the windfall profits of royalties became more and more sophisticated in the economics and politics of petroleum, partly because of investments in Western education for some of their youth. Individual countries at first bargained separately with oil companies, which were able to effectively determine prices, making only such concessions as would maintain their welcome. Even the nationalization of the Anglo-Iranian Oil Company in 1951 produced so little benefit for Iran that that course did not immediately represent an attractive prospect. In 1960, however, the oil producing nations of the Middle East and Latin America joined in the Organization of Petroleum Exporting Countries (OPEC), and began to coordinate their efforts. For nearly a decade this arrangement produced only marginal gains, as there was a sufficient excess of supply to permit the oil consumers to bargain successfully; but since 1970, as OPEC began to show a capacity to limit supply, the oil producing countries have been able to force the international oil companies into renegotiating agreements by threats of expropriation or unilateral abrogation.

The 1950's and 60's witnessed an exceedingly complex struggle for influence in the Middle East, with the Soviet Union and the United States involved in competitive wooing of the newly independent nations, while they in turn encouraged competitive bidding for concessions. In general the United States concentrated on defense arrangements, especially during the 1950's while John Foster Dulles was Secretary of State. The Baghdad Pact of this era represented a grouping of the nations on the southern flank of the Soviet Union, massively supported by the United States. The Soviet response was a growing effort at political penetration. The founding of the State of Israel in 1948 and the war that followed provided some opportunity for Soviet political maneuver. For while the United States substantially armed Iran, Turkey, Iraq and Pakistan to support the northern tier of the Baghdad Pact, it attempted to restrain the armament of Israel's neighbor states. This policy backfired in a rapid sequence of events.

An Egyptian revolution, carried out by military officers in 1952, overthrew the corrupt and ineffective British-supported monarchy and established a nationalistic military government led by a formerly obscure colonel, Gamel Abdel Nasser, whose administration pressed for internal modernization, a kind of pragmatic socialism, and external assertiveness. The principal international concerns of the new Egyptian regime were, "to liquidate the remnants of imperialism" by forcing British withdrawal from the Sudan and the Suez bases and eventually the nationalization of the Suez Canal; to assert leadership of the Arab world, leading to experiments in federation and military ventures as well as subversion; and to gain great power recognition, aid and support without falling into aligned dependency. The United States attempted to enlist this regime in its defense structure without success, and failing that, to establish cooperative anti-Soviet relations, a policy that clashed with the then popular concept of non-alignment of the newly independent state. The matter came to a head when Nasser, stung by the military response of Israel to border terrorism and unable to negotiate arms purchases with the United States, announced in September of 1955 that Egypt had bought arms from Czechoslovakia. This provoked Secretary of State Dulles to withdraw from negotiations to assist in the Aswan High Dam project, to be followed in quick succession by Nasser's nationalization of the Suez Canal Company, which was followed in turn by the Suez War of 1956, as will be further discussed below, and ended with the emergence of massive Soviet influence in the very heart of the Middle East, Egypt.

The post-World War II period saw intensified civil disorder in Palestine, including acts of terrorism by both Jew and Arab. An increasing flow of Jewish immigrants, many of them of a new type—young, educated idealists—came from all over Europe. Jewish immigration and Jewish land purchases from absentee landlords were opposed by displaced Palestinians and nationalists. There were civil disorders and riots. Commissions were mounted and white papers issued to little avail, and ultimately, under growing military pressure from both Zionist and Arab forces, the mandatory power was forced to announce its intention to withdraw. Again various commissions reviewed the problem and both the United States and the Soviet Union supported the partition of Palestine into Arab and Jewish sectors, a plan approved by the United Nations and accepted by the Jews but rejected by the Palestine Arabs and neighboring Arab States. Eight hours before the expiration of the Mandate the Jewish leader, David Ben-Gurion, read the Proclamation of Independence of the State of Israel; Israel was immediately recognized by the United States and by the Soviet Union. The progression from peoplehood to the perception of nationhood to national state had been accomplished. The next day an Egyptian plane dropped bombs on Tel Aviv and the new state was at war.

The Arab League rejected and ignored United Nations decrees; invasions of Palestine were immediately mounted by Egypt, Jordan, Syria and Lebanon; Saudi Arabia sent two battalions to serve under Egyptian Command and Iraqi forces joined the Jordanians; in addition, irregular forces were organized under Palestinian leadership as an Arab Liberation Army. Despite this listing, the actual numbers of Arab forces were modest; no more than 100,000 were ever engaged in the campaign which, moreover, lacked unified plans or command and was fought, with few exceptions, by inexperienced and unenthusiastic soldiers. The armed forces of Israel, by contrast, were highly organized and led by officers who had battle training with the British and combat experience from the Second World War. The outcome was a temporary occupation of previously Arab populated territories by the invading armies while the Israeli forces defeated the invaders in a series of offensives interspersed by temporary truces; the armistice agreements signed separately with the Arab states between February and July 1949 found Israel in possession of substantially all the former mandate territory except for some enclaves on the Jordanian side of the Jordan River that had been taken and subsequently evacuated in consequence of the armistice agreements by the Syrians; the West Bank of the Jordan and old Jerusalem, which were annexed by Jordan; and the Gaza Strip, occupied but not annexed by Egypt.

By the end of Israel's war of independence the local actors in the Middle East conflict, which has continued for over 25 years, were well defined. The immediate antagonists were Israel and the neighboring Arab states of Egypt, Jordan, Syria and Lebanon; each of these was post-colonial and soon to engage in its particular version of modernizing revolutionary change—in fact, the changes were stimulated by the conflict and sometimes by the example of Israel. Initially, the Palestine Arabs were for the most part refugees, their nationalist hopes shattered and their leaders demoralized; but they gradually developed into an active force which presaged a perception of nationhood. Deprived of the territorial base for the statehood toward which it increasingly aspired, and which the U.N. Partition Plan had originally promised, Palestine Arab nationalism became the Arab equivalent of Zionism before Israel was proclaimed and has since followed a similar course of development, gradually acquiring the elements of organization and governance, irregular military capability and international sponsors and influence, always seeking the establishment of a state in Palestine. Meanwhile, Israel, despite constant conflict and four wars with its neighbors in a quarter century, has managed to develop a democratic national state.

The accomplishments of Israel include the ingathering and integration of hundreds of thousands of Jews from all corners of the earth, the rapid development of modern industrial and agricultural capacities adapted to the peculiar conditions of the country, the establishment of modern educational and technological institutions, attraction of massive economic support from world Jewry, military capabilities—including the ability to mobilize the entire facilities of the nation to war purposes—and global diplomatic relations. The nation which began with a population of 650,000 has grown to over three million, including nearly half a million Arabs, and since 1967, has administered territories occupied by a million more. What Israel has not been able to do is find a way to peace with her Arab neighbors.

The particular character of Israel society, including the determination of her people never again to rely heavily on promises of other peoples and nations to ensure the security of Jews; the unfortunate and unresolved status of Palestinian Arabs as a people with a perception of nationhood; the problems of pride and geography which Israel presents to her Arab neighbors; all have contributed to a continuing state of conflict which has inevitably meshed with the international interests intersecting in the region. The consequence has been gradually deepening international involvement in the conflicts of the area; the United States, having both sentimental and strategic commitments to Israel, has been less than successful in sustaining relations with the Arab countries of the Middle East; the Soviet Union gradually established political footholds in Arab states by supporting their cause politically and with arms; France and England have wavered from side to side in terms of their perceived interests; China has found it useful to support radical groups in Yemen and among the Palestinians in terms of its policy of support for armed popular struggles against imperialist powers. More recently the Arab application of the "oil weapon" found oil-dependent states from Japan to Europe, from Africa to Latin America compelled to give at least lip-service support to Arab aspirations. In brief, a broad range of international interests have come to focus on the Arab-Israeli conflict, which has thus become a world as well as a regional problem.

The first Arab-Israeli war was seen by Israelis as a war of independence, cementing the establishment of the state; subsequent wars have been seen as wars of survival of the national state. For the Arabs, the first war was an expression of national assertion; thereafter, a complex of motives prevented Arab leadership from ending the state of belligerency. New pride and dignity in their perception of nationhood, support for the claim of Palestinian brother Arabs to return home, competition for leadership, or at least acceptance in the Arab world, social mobilization of the national peoples to face an enemy, desire to build military

forces as instruments of governance and respect; these motives played a major part in the Arab states' continuing refusal to end the state of war or to negotiate a peace, especially
as Israel's best terms could not resolve the issues.

The Arab belligerents imposed a boycott on trade and
communication, including the use of the Suez Canal by Israeli ships or cargoes intended for Israel; they uttered
threats against Israel's survival and promises of ultimate war;
they permitted or encouraged border raids and acts of terror
by Palestinians and Arab volunteers. All these activities grew
in intensity after Nasser's revolution; it became clear that
revolutionary nationalism prospered from the presence of
an enemy, as well as from repudiation of any external intervention, and other nations followed suit. While these activities were popular with Arab citizens, they caused increasing
tension in Israel, especially as Nasser emerged as a dominant
figure in the Arab world.

After Egypt nationalized the Suez Canal in 1956, thereby
precipitating an international crisis, the Israeli cabinet decided that war was inevitable and entered into a secret
agreement with Great Britain and France, who, in the last
throes of imperial reaction, were in any event looking for a
"casus belli." On October 29, 1956, Israeli forces, led by
tanks, invaded the Sinai and rapidly swept to the Suez Canal
in an action which met little effective resistance. Britain and
France launched air attacks on Suez. The United Nations,
including the United States and the Soviet Union, condemned this attack and the Soviet Union threatened nuclear
intervention, whereupon France and Great Britain withdrew. Under heavy and almost universal international pressure, Israel agreed to withdraw from Sinai and a United
Nations force was established on the border with Egypt and
at Sharm el Sheikh, which controls the Straits of Tiran.
Nasser was not toppled, Egyptian recognition and ending of
belligerency was not achieved, and further fuel was added to

Arab hostility to Israel. Egypt's military defeat thus ended
in a political victory.

Subsequent to the Sinai War two major factors entered the
equation of the Middle East conflict. The Soviet Union consolidated her political relations with Egypt, Syria, and Iraq,
paying the price of providing very substantial modern
armaments; this was countered by United States provision of
a balance of arms to Israel and support for Jordan. The
second factor was the emergence of the Palestine Arabs as an
organized political and military force, explicitly committed to
the goal of establishing a Palestinian state, preferably on the
territory of their former "homeland," now occupied by Israel. These factors contributed to an escalating level of terrorism and harassment of the borders of Israel, which responded with a declared policy of retaliatory military raids
on guerrilla bases with deliberate destruction of homes and
property.

The crisis and war of 1967 grew out of the tensions engendered by Palestinian commando raids and Israel's reaction. The raids were mounted by Palestinian commandos
organized in some ten political groupings. Al Fatah, the
largest, had been founded in Stuttgart in the 1950's by three
Palestinian refugee students, including Yasir Arafat. In the
1960's they organized military groups which were often
trained in radical Arab countries such as Algeria. The first Al
Fatah commando raid was carried out in 1965, and by the
end of 1966 they and other groups were mounting small-
scale but effective military raids from Jordan, Syria, and
Lebanon while the government and people of Israel became
increasingly tense and frustrated. In November, regular Israeli forces carried out a major retaliatory raid on the Jordanian village of Al-Samu; a number of Jordanian soldiers and
civilians were killed and wounded, and systematic destruction was carried out. The United Nations condemned the
action in the Security Council. Palestinian commando raids

continued and were increasingly encouraged and justified by the governments of Syria, Jordan and Egypt.

As the crisis deepened in the spring of 1967, the Soviet Union joined in denunciations of Israeli actions and in May accused Israel of planning a pre-emptive war and massing troops. Egypt responded by building up its military forces in Sinai as a show of strength, and on May 17 Nasser requested the United Nations to remove its Emergency Forces from the Sinai armistice line. The Secretary General ordered their withdrawal, including those in Sharm el Sheikh. While subsequent history has shown that nobody wanted a war at this time, the crisis grew beyond control, and after Egypt sought to re-establish its blockade of the Straits of Tiran, the Israeli government concluded that it was in danger of attack on several fronts and that, in any case, an act of war had been committed. On June 5, 1967, Israeli forces pre-emptively struck simultaneously at Syria and at Egyptian positions in the Sinai; Jordan reluctantly attacked in support of its fellow Arab states, and contingents from Iraq and other Arab states were dispatched to the front. The Israelis destroyed the Egyptian Air Force on the ground—and after six days of savage fighting, Israeli forces again occupied Sinai to the Suez Canal, the Golan Heights of Syria, and the West Bank of the Jordan, as well as the Old City of Jerusalem. There the cease-fire lines were drawn. Arab threats to destroy Israel, combined with Soviet miscalculation in efforts to establish a Middle East foothold, and United States vacillation, had produced what Israel regarded as a critical security threat which was reduced by a whirlwind Israeli military victory and attainment of what came to be defined as "natural defensible borders."

The conclusion of the June War did not bring peace. The humiliated Arab states were not inclined to negotiate unless Israel agreed to withdraw from occupied Arab territory; to do so, they said, would be to accept Israel's possession of what was already theirs. Nasser offered to resign the presidency of Egypt but was persuaded to continue his mission. An Arab summit meeting in Khartoum at the end of August decided on a position of "no peace, no negotiation, and no recognition" of Israel. Israel refused to withdraw from her "more defensible borders" without direct negotiation and an end to the state of Arab belligerency. Once again the demands of Israel for territorial security and of the Arabs for "dignity" and "justice" produced a deadlock. The state of conflict continued unabated.

The alarmed international community debated the issues and, in November, Security Council Resolution 242 was approved at the United Nations. This called "for a just and lasting peace in which every state in the area can live in security" and laid down principles of "withdrawal of Israeli armed forces from territories occupied in the recent conflict," termination of states of belligerency, and "acknowledgment of the sovereignty, territorial integrity, and political independence of every State in the area." A United Nations mediator was appointed but no progress was made in breaking the deadlock. Meanwhile, the Soviet Union began a massive rearmament of Egypt and Syria and the United States again responded by providing Israel with sufficient arms to maintain its military strength, or what many observers would consider her military advantage.

For the next six years an exceedingly complex pattern of interaction ensued, essentially a condition of continued conflict with neither peace nor international war, leading to ever-widening circles of international involvement. Israel consolidated her new defense lines and enjoyed, for the first time, a sense of relative security, meanwhile following a policy of firmness and considerable restraint in administering the occupied territories, even maintaining a semi-open border with Jordan. However, two new factors soon disturbed this security: the rising levels of organization and activity of

Palestine Arab forces, especially their resort to international terrorism as a technique for commanding world attention; and the process of a war of attrition by neighboring states, especially Egypt, drawing increasing support from wealthy Arab states not bordering Israel.

The defeat of Arab forces in 1967 thoroughly demoralized the Palestinian refugees, or exiles, as they had begun to call themselves. But out of that demoralization grew a new realization and determination. The realization was that Israel was entrenched beyond hope of foreseeable displacement and that they could not rely on the Arab states to recover their homeland for them. The determination was to turn to direct action toward the assertion of independent nation-hood with the purpose of establishing a national state. The Palestine Liberation Organization (PLO) began to function as the central spokesman for the would-be liberators of Pales-tine and was able to attract funds from oil producing Arab states and arms from the Soviet Union and, in the case of more radical factions, from China. Palestinian military units were formed in the territories of Jordan, Syria and Lebanon and soon became forces to be reckoned with in those coun-tries, growing steadily more independent of national gov-ernments.

While Palestinian military forces were being formed by the larger and more conventional elements of the PLO, more radical factions began a campaign of international terror in the summer of 1968—a campaign sometimes disowned but never disavowed by the PLO. The first targets were Israeli: El Al airplanes were attacked, markets were bombed, shoot-ings and kidnappings were carried out against Israeli offi-cials. The campaign soon spread to hijacking and destruction of planes of international air carriers, the most dramatic incident being the September 1970 simultaneous hijacking of a Pan Am jet to Egypt, as well as TWA and Swissair planes to Jordan, and their destruction after negotiating the release of

guerrillas detained in Zurich. These and other terrorist attacks, including the massacre at Tel Aviv's Lod Airport by
radical Japanese terrorists and the murder of eleven Israeli
athletes at Olympic Village in Munich in September 1972,
certainly succeeded in dramatizing the presence and determination of Palestinians as an independent force in the Middle East. To underline the lesson, Palestinian military forces
in Jordan defied the authority of King Hussein in 1970 and
were suppressed only after bloody battles with the Jordanian
army.

On the Egyptian-Israeli cease-fire line along the Suez
Canal, another kind of pressure erupted with major artillery
bombardments by Egypt and Israeli replies, beginning in
September 1968. An Egyptian "war of attrition" had begun
which was to intensify to serious levels of air warfare until a
cease-fire was finally arranged in August 1970, in terms of
proposals made by the United States Secretary of State William P. Rogers. President Nasser died soon afterward, however, and although his successor, Anwar el-Sadat, renewed
the cease fire, he began a diplomatic offensive, and at other
times threatened to launch a war.

The effect of these events was to increase the levels and
intensity of diplomatic maneuver, with the United Nations
special representative and the United States Secretary of
State and President playing increasingly active roles, while
the intensity of bilateral talks increased between the Soviet
Union and the United States on one hand, and the Soviet
Union and Arab leaders on the other. However, the relative
positions remained fixed—Arab neighbors refused to
negotiate unless Israel withdrew to the pre-1967 lines and
Israel refused to consider withdrawals without peace negotiations. Meanwhile terrorism and border raids continued,
while Egypt's Sadat solemnly threatened to attack across
Suez, whatever the cost, unless there should be some progress in recovery of territory. Military estimates considered

such an action unlikely of success, especially since Sadat had requested the Soviet Union to withdraw its military missions in June 1972 and subsequent arms deliveries had slowed. A build-up in 1973 was not regarded seriously. Moreover, the Soviet-American movement of detente seemed to place restraints on great power support for any attack.

Suddenly, on October 6, 1973, Egypt and Syria mounted attacks on Israel's borders, secretly prepared but long announced by Sadat. Both attacks were initially successful. Egyptian soldiers crossed Suez on pontoon bridges and breached the Bar-Lev defense lines, a military accomplishment that had been inconceivable to Israel's military analysts. Egyptian units launched a massive tank attack on the defended passes in the Sinai. Israeli air superiority was substantially neutralized by effective Egyptian missile and anti-aircraft defenses. At the same time, Syrian tank-infantry attacks overwhelmed Israeli border forces, and they too demonstrated unexpected capability with anti-tank and artillery weapons. For several days Israel was on the defensive while her reserves were mobilized. Subsequently, the tide of battle turned, first on the Syrian front as Israeli tanks, troops, and artillery pushed, against fierce resistance, toward Damascus; then on the Sinai front, where Israeli forces penetrated across the Suez Canal and threatened the rear of the Egyptian beachhead. On the sixteenth day of warfare, a cease-fire in place was effected by United Nations demand. The Soviet Union had delayed in joining this demand until it became evident that there was a strong possibility of a major Egyptian defeat. After breaches on the Egyptian front involving the entrapment of an Egyptian army and its negotiated extrication in a symbolically important meeting between Israeli and Egyptian field commanders under United Nations auspices, the fighting ceased. And in January, 1974, after active and protracted shuttle diplomacy by United States Secretary of State Henry Kissinger, a disengagement of forces and the interposition of United Nations Forces was agreed to. Egypt retained possession of the east bank of Suez and the canal's clearance was agreed to. Israel had extended and retained its Golan salient.

More important than the immediate outcome, however, were the effects of the 1973 war on the national participants, their supporters, and the international community. As will be apparent in the reports of interviews with individual citizens, the people and government of Israel were decidedly sobered and have, ever since, undertaken a reappraisal of their previous assumptions concerning their international position and especially concerning their Arab adversaries. The Arabs, by contrast, experienced a new self-respect arising from their military successes and the demonstrations of competence and self-sufficiency as individuals and as societies; as a consequence, they too have undertaken a reappraisal of their position vis-á-vis Israel, particularly as this has been articulated by President Sadat of Egypt, although the same basic demands remain.

The effects of the 1973 war were profound on other levels as well. Perhaps of greatest importance was a new cooperation among Arab states, regardless of internal political orientation. Jordan sent only token forces to the Syrian front and Iraq not much more, but a new level of support appeared in the form of political backing by all the Arab nations and the imposition of an oil embargo by each of the Arab oil-producing states. Most notable was Saudi Arabia, which had previously maintained a U.S.-oriented and relatively conservative position, but which during the conflict clamped an effective embargo on oil deliveries to the United States. It was only in retrospect that the Western nations discovered that Egypt had brought Saudi Arabia's leadership into its planning long before the attack. Arab loyalty proved stronger than sympathetic ties to the West, especially, perhaps, when long-range economic advantage could be gained. However strange a partnership between conservative Saudi Arabia and radical socialist Syria might appear, we are reminded of an ancient Arab proverb, "My brother and I against our cousin, my cousin and I against the stranger." In any event, the capacity for cooperation, at least in respect to conflict with Israel, has been apparent ever since and has profoundly altered Arab self-images and outside powers' assumptions.

Israel, too, discovered secondary ties of significance. Even as a sense of international isolation increased, the response of world Jewry to the threat to Israel's existence was immediate and unexpected by Israeli officials. Jews in England and the United States, Europe, and Latin America expressed a new level of support for Israel, economically, politically, and for many Jews in a willingness to come and fight, if necessary, for Israel's survival. Clearly, the single most important international friend of Israel was the United States; the war quickly showed that the idea of a small nation standing alone and being able to sustain modern capacities for warfare was a romantic myth, and that Israel's future would also depend on cooperative international relations, and perhaps more importantly, on the strong support of a superpower.

The 1973 Arab offensive could only be mounted with Soviet knowledge and agreement. Obviously the Soviet government had decided on an adventurous policy in the Middle East, one that continued with high level appeals by the Soviet leadership to other Arab states to join the hostilities, with threats, written and explicit, to intervene unilaterally with Soviet forces to prevent a major defeat of Egypt during the cease-fire crisis, and the assumption of a high risk of military confrontation with the U.S. The United States responded uncertainly at first but then with great firmness, finally mounting a direct military airlift of military supplies to Israel in the form, for the first time, of direct gifts and diplomatically warning the Soviet Union of the risks of intervention; even putting American military forces on world-wide alert. There was no longer any doubt of the potential of the Middle East conflict to precipitate a great power confrontation or even war. In the event, the two great powers drew back from confrontation and jointly agreed to sponsor a search for negotiated peace. An era of negotiation on the region had finally come, no matter how uncertain its course and outcome; negotiation that involved not only the combatants but the second tier of Arab countries and, with undeniable commitment, the United States and Soviet Union.

We will not review the course of international negotiation since the 1973 war. Suffice it to say that the U.S. Secretary of State played a principal role as mediator, in indirect negotiations, between Israel and Egypt specifically, but involving the other Arab states as well. The hope was to gain step by step reciprocal agreement until direct negotiations could be begun—as had been agreed with the first disengagement. Meanwhile, the United States rearmed Israel and the Soviet Union rearmed Syria and Egypt. The main issues are security, recognition, and ending of belligerency for Israel; return of occupied territories and some sort of satisfaction of Palestine Arab aspirations for the Arabs; the details are infinitely complex.

Finally, we return again to the Palestine Arabs, whose fate and actions have constituted a central problem in the conflict and continue to do so. Their number approaches three million—more than one million living in Israel or in Israeli-occupied territory; 600,000 still in the refugee camps of Lebanon, Syria and Jordan. Most of the remainder are dispersed through the Arab world, often in positions of considerable influence, because, among the most skilled and best educated of the Arab elite, many are Palestinians. Despite the early recommendations of the United Nations for repatriation or resettlement of Palestinians, neither has occurred. Fewer former Arab inhabitants of Palestine have changed their identity; many have found a sense of national identity in exile that scarcely existed heretofore. Most subscribe to

Article 5 of the PLO Covenant: "The Palestinians are the Arab Citizens who were living permanently in Palestine until 1947, whether they were expelled from there or remained; whoever is born to a Palestinian Arab father after this date, within Palestine or outside it, is a Palestinian."

Palestinian forces fought in Syria during the 1973 war and shared in defeat; the almost immediate response was a doubling of determination and drive toward organization and assertion of independent identity. The international terrorist attacks by radical factions continued, but a new sort appeared as well. Suicide terror squads—soldiers and heroes to the Palestinians—penetrated into Israel and seized hostages. They have invariably been killed or captured, and many civilian hostages have died with them. They continue to keep the Palestinian issue before the world. As soon as the era of negotiations began, the Palestinians expressed a fear of being squeezed out of any negotiated settlement and emphasized their independent interests and policy within the Arab world, a process that has led the PLO to de-emphasize terrorist tactics and even denounce and offer to try to punish irregular terrorist activities such as the murder of the United States Ambassador to the Sudan in 1974. Intense political and diplomatic activity in the Arab world led to recognition of the PLO as the Palestinian authority at an Arab summit meeting in Rabat in October 1974. Immediately afterward, the PLO leader, Yasir Arafat, addressed the General Assembly of the United Nations, the first time that any organization other than a recognized government has done so. The Palestine Arabs thereby achieved some international recognition of their claim to nationhood; they avowedly seek statehood and insist, with some success, that they be officially represented in any general peace negotiations that are undertaken.

In this review we have outlined some of the complex forces that enter into the conflict in the Middle East; even then we have only touched on the principal trends, issues, and events which have affected the region and the course of conflict. We have neglected the micro-politics of the particular nations, including the impact of personality of individual leaders, which at times has not been negligible, and we have only alluded to the macro-politics of international policy and diplomatic relations that have borne upon the nations and peoples of the area. These fundamental and persisting realities of history and geography, power and resource, play a great role in the actions of nations; in fact, they substantially determine the possibilities open to them.

The second set of fundamental realities has grown out of nationalism, the search for equality and dignity, recognition and security of peoples through their achievement of national statehood. The simultaneous rise of Jewish and Arab nationalism in the Middle East, and the chain of events that led to the displacement of Palestinian Arabs provided a basis for regional conflict which has been deeply intertwined and mutually interactive with the clash of great power interests in the area to produce a protracted conflict and four wars in a single generation. As we turn to the level of participation of individual citizens in the conflicts of their nations, we will examine the degree to which these "wars begin in the minds of men," in the involvement of the self in fears and hopes for the nation.

References

1. Karl W. Deutsch. NATIONALISM AND ITS ALTERNATIVES (New York: Alfred A. Knopf, 1969).
2. Hans Kohn. THE AGE OF NATIONALISM (New York: Harper and Brothers, 1962) p 86. See also George Antonius, THE ARAB AWAKENING (Beirut: Khayats, 1942).
3. Atallah Mansour. "Palestine and the Search for a New Golden Age," in ISRAEL AND THE PALESTINIANS, Shlomo Avineri, ed (New York: St. Martin's Press, 1971) p 88.

3

THE PALESTINE ARABS: NARCISSISTIC RAGE AND THE SEARCH FOR SELF-ESTEEM

The material for this chapter is drawn from interviews conducted between 1960 and 1975. Interviews in Israel, the neighboring Arab countries and refugee camps were conducted in 1960, 1970, and 1972, and in the United States at intervals throughout the period. Notes recorded after these interviews provide the basis for most of this report. As much as possible we have allowed the material to speak for itself, organizing observations in terms of the phases that emerged from our data. Our interview subjects are not a complete cross-section of Palestinians, but they do reflect "soundings" of the Palestinian universe. We have not analyzed either the political structures or the refugee experience, as these are special cases better studied by other methods.

Four distinct stages in the development of political self-consciousness on the part of the Palestinians have been observed: they can be described as a stage of *peoplehood*, roughly from 1916–1955; a sense of *nationalistic peoplehood*, from 1955–1967; the perception of *nationhood*, which can be said to have been achieved in October 1974; and the movement toward *statehood*, which many would contend has become manifest since 1974. Although these stages overlap and each has much earlier precedents, we base these descriptions on the state of political awareness, and to some extent, of organization of the majority of Palestinian people.

We do not intend to enter into the intimate history of the Palestinian people or into the historic claims and counter-claims made concerning the legitimacy of national statehood, for we are acutely aware of narcissistic investment in the history of peoples and that, even now, the Palestinian people are reconstructing their own historic record. In fact, argument on this subject has been intense, with Palestinian partisans pressing the record further and further back—how many times have we been shown antique volumes in which European missionaries or adventurers wrote of the "Palestine people" over several centuries—while Zionist partisans have been at pains to insist that Palestine did not exist as a political or national entity and that its inhabitants did not view themselves as a nation, both sides selectively quoting from the historic record and engaging at times in a high level of invective. Nothing more clearly represents the levels of self-involvement in nations than the passion with which the instruments of scholarship and debate have been applied to the subject.

For at least the 3,000 years of recorded history, various groups of people have inhabited the levantine littoral, organized as tribes and clans but always surviving as local subject peoples. This long experience of subject peoplehood, with rule by vastly superior force, encouraged a political culture of localism. The *millet* system of the Ottoman Empire, that organized its subjects into religious communities ruled in civil and religious affairs by their own clerics, but gave them no voice whatsoever in the policies of empire, greatly reinforced this tendency as well as a certain distrust of government—700 years of such rule preceded the first World War.

Under the Mandate, the sense of peoplehood gained strength and Palestinian Arabs began to resist the mandatory authority and, later, Jewish immigration that displaced them from their lands. Massive "spontaneous" riots in Jaffa in

1936 marked the beginning of disturbances that continued
to 1948; later, Palestinian leaders organized a general strike
and formed a Higher Arab Committee to coordinate their
resistance. Paradoxically, it was the establishment of the state
of Israel and the subsequent displacement of more than
700,000 Palestinian Arabs from their homes and country of
Palestine that fully crystallized the sense of peoplehood, a
feeling of common history, culture and fate distinct from
other Arab peoples, a sense that has come to be asserted with
increasing intensity. Indeed, the more the Western powers
and Israel proposed resettlement and assumed that Palestinians might melt into the wider Arab world, the more
strongly did the sense of distinct Palestinian identity emerge;
a deeper common bond was forged by the experience of
refugeeism which soon became defined as exile.

By the beginning of 1975, an estimated 3.2 million people
considered themselves Arab Palestinians in their fundamental political identity and sense of national loyalty, regardless
of where they lived and what passports they carried. They
were widely dispersed: 470,000 lived in Israel with rights of
citizenship; 640,000 on the West Bank of the Jordan and
390,000 in the Gaza area—both under Israeli occupation
since the June War of 1967; 320,000 in Lebanon where the
organized Palestinian military forces were actually larger
than the Lebanese Army of 12,000; 900,000 more in Jordan
on the East Bank of the Jordan River—their number and
military freedom of movement having been reduced by their
suppression by the Jordanian Army in 1970; another
200,000 in Syria where organized forces were closely integrated with those of Syria; and at least a quarter million in
Saudi Arabia, the Emirates, Iraq and Kuwait—in these places
often in roles as teachers, technicians, and administrators.
The level of education and technical training among
Palestinians is uniquely high among Arab peoples (about
75,000 university graduates). They are in great demand in the

modernizing Arab World. Additionally, tens of thousands of Palestinian youth are temporarily sojourning in the major capitals and university centers of the world, from Moscow to Washington.

By 1975, the chief political organization of the Palestinians, the Palestine Liberation Organization, had been recognized at the Rabat Conference by eighteen Arab states and Emirates, who accepted its chairman, Yasir Arafat, as the sole legitimate spokesman for all Palestinians, having rebuffed the claims of King Hussein of Jordan to that role. Arafat had spoken to the General Assembly of the United Nations as the first non-state representative to do so; he had met with principal French diplomats, and in March of 1975 with the United States Senator, George McGovern. Thus, while they still lack an internationally recognized government and a territory of their own, the Palestinian Arab people have achieved a feeling of nationhood and aspire to statehood. Indeed, a number of states—principally the third world countries—have accorded the Palestinian people many of the signs of recognition usually reserved for national states.

Palestinian rage and sense of national identity

"We are not Egyptians," a young man said in Gaza in 1960, "we are Palestinians." "Yes, we are Arabs, but first of all, we are Palestinians." Another young Palestinian interviewed in Jericho in the same year was more emphatic: "Most of all I am not Jordanian. Although I carry a Jordan passport, I do not like it." And in the village of Rama, in Israel, a student spoke, "Of course I'm Palestinian, I'm not Israeli. They let us stay here where we've always lived—my great-grandfather built this house. And I have many friends among the Jews, but I am Arab, I am Palestinian. They let us stay, but it is like the caged bird. When the wild bird envies his well-being, he thinks, 'You envy me my food but you do not see the bars.' "

By that year, 1960, a large majority of the Palestine Arab population had established a distinctive Palestine Arab identity and sense of peoplehood; indeed, they had entered a phase of what might be termed *nationalistic* peoplehood with the simple but definite goal of "return to our homes in Palestine." The young men whose comments we have quoted—which could be extended a thousandfold—asserted their uniquely Palestinian identity positively and vigorously, especially asserting what they were not, identities they rejected.

A series of systematic interviews was carried out at that time with Palestinian Arabs in refugee camps in Gaza and Jordan, in Arab cities of Cairo and Jerusalem, and in Arab villages in Israel. As we will see, a powerful element in the expressions of the subjects was that of narcissistic rage, expressed as much or more freely for the Palestinian people as for the self. This rage, which arose out of a sense of injury and shame, insult, subjection to intrusion and terrorist violence, and ultimate disinheritance, shared the features described by Kohut as occurring among patients who had suffered such injury: "The need for revenge, for righting a wrong, for undoing a hurt by whatever means, and a deeply anchored, unrelenting compulsion in the pursuit of all these aims which gives no rest to those who have suffered a narcissistic injury . . ." It is notable that this emotion was expressed, sometimes with a sense of intense psychological pain, by self-identified Palestinians who were doing very well materially in their personal lives, as well as by those who inhabited refugee camps. It was also notable that the subjects shared another characteristic of this condition noted by Kohut: ". . . the reasoning capacity, while totally under the domination and in the service of the overriding emotion, is often not only intact but even sharpened."[1]

We will quote a series of statements made by different subjects. Later we shall review the background of the Palestin-

ian Arab people and provide examples of changes in psychological state with the evolution of a sense of Palestinian
national identity. The sense of nationalistic peoplehood and
of narcissistic rage extended roughly from 1954, following
the shock of defeat and flight, to about 1968, when actions
arising out of rage attracted world attention and may have
begun a process of resolution of rage, partly by the shift from
passive-helpless identity to active-aggressive self-image,
partly from the attention of powerful outsiders and partly
from the achievement of broader recognition in the thrust
for nationhood. We do not mean to imply that nationalistic
feelings and rage did not occur before this phase of Palestinian history or that narcissistic rage has disappeared since,
but only that this was a principal theme of a particular stage
of the development of the people.

The mayor of a refugee camp near Jericho spoke with
dignity and sorrow; he is Christian but his first act as mayor
was to organize the building of a mosque for his people.
"Our land was near Beersheba; would you like to see the
deeds? We prospered and we were not disturbed. Then came
the Jews and they brought war. We did not fight, we wanted
only to keep our land and our homes. I took my people into
the country while the police and the Egyptians tried to hold
Beersheba. When they were beaten and withdrew I went to
the Jewish commander and asked to be allowed to stay on
our land and live in peace. His answer came in armored cars;
we had to leave at once. It was the 21st of October, 1948, a
day my people will never forget. It is cold in the mountains in
winter and we had no shelter. So we came down into this
warm valley by the Dead Sea and here we've stayed. We wait
for justice. We do not like to live without work. We are proud
but there is nothing we can do. An Arab is wedded to his land
and mine is near Beersheba. Some day justice will come to
us." At this point, an old man, who was listening, angrily
interjected, "Justice lies in the blood of Jewish thieves. I'll

drink the blood of a hundred Jews before my justice is done. My land, my dignity and my life are gone. Where is the justice for that?"

A young man in a refugee village in the Gaza strip could not restrain himself, "We will kill Jews! Since I was eight I have planned it. There are many of us. The guns will come from Russia when the time is ripe. Yes, we will have our land—America, our enemy, will be fighting its own war and will not be able to protect its Jewish friends. I wait for that day." And his headman explained, "I do not know what will happen when we old ones are gone. We restrain our sons now, but they are bitter and they have no judgment. Sometimes even I wonder if they aren't right.

Four young men in Gaza, not refugees but young men of property, shared their fantasy of grandiose omnipotence, "Yes, I am rich, but I have no rights. You see, I have no state. Do you know what it is like to be a stateless person? It is slavery. I must ask the Egyptians when I can come or go. It is in our minds and it will never leave, that someday, somehow, we will have our country again and can lift our heads again. Our country is Palestine." The second, "I will be mayor of Tel Aviv when the Jews are gone. They will go like this" —crushing a cigarette box with a mighty smash. The third, "It is true that I'm a policeman now. But a policeman learns much and a police lieutenant now is an army general tomorrow. It is I who will make my friend mayor of Tel Aviv. We have our plans—you will learn them when we strike." And the last, "I do not look beyond the war to come. I do not want to be a general or a mayor although we need them. What I want is a gun to shoot the thieves. For that it is best to be a private in the army. That is all I want to be, a soldier with a gun, and that is what I will be."

The identity formation begins early; a boy of eight born in exile: "My home is Nazareth. I've never seen it, but I know it all because my parents tell me every day—I won't forget. My father had four sewing machines; his business was good and we were happy. The thieves stole it all. They killed my uncle. Someday I will go home."

There was little variation except in details and in expressive style: Palestinian professors in New York, students in Cairo, businessmen in Damascus related identical themes. Finally, a major Palestinian leader, highly educated, spoke in tempered tones, "It's a question of power. The Americans back the Zionists because they control so much of the economic life of America. We are used to that because that was true in Britain too. They speak with a powerful voice to your government. However we, too, have power and we are getting more. The Arab people control oil, without which you cannot live. Our Palestinians throughout the Arab world are organizing in a unified way to use this power. When we have gained it you will see the consequences of your policy. It is a question of survival of the fittest. The Jews were more fit before, tougher, better organized. But we will grow in strength—our exile makes us tougher. When will the showdown come? With World War III; then the Palestine problem will be settled on the battlefields of Palestine. We wait for that day. In fact we will, if necessary, be the ones who start that war. You talk of peace, but we know the truth that only war will give us our country and our state—war and nothing else."

The comments we have quoted were frequently discounted as some sort of political product of Arab propagandist manipulation, but it was obvious to anyone with direct contact with the subjects that deeply felt emotions were being expressed. The intensity of emotional expression, and even more impressively, the struggle for self-control among the more restrained spokesmen—and by 1960 virtually every Palestinian regarded himself as a spokesman for his people when confronted by an outsider—bore the unmistakable signs of genuine, personal, implacable rage. The feeling communicated itself readily to other Arabs, and often to Europeans who had contact with Palestinians. A colonel of the Army of the United Arab Republic who had control responsibilities in the Gaza Strip and who was in frequent conflict with its inhabitants nevertheless sympathized, "The Palestinians will never rest until they regain their homes. They cannot be resettled, for they remain strangers in foreign lands. They cannot be themselves . . . We sympathize. Someday they will return."

At this point, some preliminary comments and assessments are indicated. Questions have been raised as to whether the Palestinian culture of childrearing practices might have produced some propensity toward a narcissistic vulnerability and undue rage reaction. Without answering this question, we would prefer to stress the fact that their intense localism left Palestinian society and the Palestinian people singularly unprepared for the events that befell them. There was no channel for response, where loyalties and responsibilities traditionally went no farther than family and clan. Coupled with this was the complete un-reachability of the offending object, Israel, to the refugees, a condition which intensified the level of rage, as did the narcissistic disacknowledgment—not taking them seriously—by the people and press of Israel and of the wider world to which they were exceedingly sensitive. By contrast, the Palestinians who remained in Israeli territory and were in direct contact with the enemy were much less afflicted by rage—they quarreled and received acknowledgment, even negative recognition of their existence. Hence, while they shared fully the ideas of Palestinian dignity and sense of nationhood, they were less outraged by their position; this was, in fact, more analogous to pre-independence Algerian rage with respect to France than the implacable raging of involuntary exile.

In this chapter, we do not intend to explore the problems of interaction between the adversary peoples, but it is obvious that the Palestinian voice was heard in Israel and that a vast quantity of psychological and political energy was devoted to denying it. In brief, the quality of rage contained the stimulus to its disacknowledgment—it was simply too primitive and too threatening which, in turn, added to its intensity.

The concept of Palestinian nationhood

The perception of nationalism, the idea of a state rooted in common consent and supported by full participation of a people, grew out of the demoralization of displacement and exile. The idea of a Palestine nation, as we have seen, was considerably older among leaders, but translating that idea into a popular sentiment required a massive transformation of the entire political culture from the ancient habits of leadership from above to new forms of active participation of the people in the formation of their society. A distinct movement toward the rise of Palestinian nationalism can be identified, but no single personality is directly responsible. Rather, the entire people, whether in exile or in the "internal exile" of living in a state dominated by another people, evolved a consensus of history and of purpose; the purpose was at first simple—"return to our homes"—but grew rapidly into a yearning for self-determination, to become a nation. Older leaders, still speaking in the United Nations, suddenly sounded dated, for the people were ahead of their leaders; it was clear that a new leadership would need to arise. And it did. Younger leaders formed groups, often of mixed political and military nature. By 1964 ten embryonic commando or guerrilla groups of diverse philosophy but a common cause were brought together in the Palestine Liberation Organization, which was to become the recognized spokesman for Palestine interests a decade later. These groups began to engage in political training and commando raids, but they and the majority of Palestinian people still looked to the other Arab states to win their cause. The habits of dependency die hard. The June War of 1967 brought another sharp change to the evolution of Palestinian national consciousness.

Two events precipitated the shift from a shared perception of nationalistic peoplehood to an emergent sense of nationhood. First, the massive defeat of the Arab states actually liberated Palestinians from reliance on them and resulted in a realization that the Palestinian people would have to seize their own initiative in their own cause. As a result, the culture of subjection and of dependency could be abandoned. Second, and almost immediately, the campaign of terror and unconventional warfare, mounted by various factions of the PLO, demonstrated to the Palestinian people that they could gain world attention almost independently of other Arab advocates. Indeed, the independent action brought considerable Arab attention and a sort of grudging recognition by Arab nations and some others that the Palestinians had not experienced before. Among the many encounters along the Israeli borders with Jordan, Syria, and Lebanon, the battle of Karameh on March 21, 1968, assumed the status of an important historic event. Israeli toops with air cover mounted an attack on an Al-Fatah stronghold near the Jordan River, and Palestinian defenders held their positions for twelve hours before they retreated, leaving some damaged Israeli tanks on the battlefield. Palestinian consciousness took a new turn, incorporating enhanced self-esteem. Recruits flocked to join commando forces, and the PLO developed a much stronger political voice. The capacity to form, support and enforce a common will, which we have noted as the hallmark of nationhood, began to emerge.

Quasi-national status was conferred upon the PLO by the Arab leadership in October, 1974, following the shifts in alignment and in support that followed the October war of 1973, especially with the political acceptance of the Palestin-

ian cause by Saudi Arabia. Immediately, the movement
toward Palestinian statehood, a subject which had been long
and hotly debated during the preceding period, assumed a
new meaning and importance. Still, the territory and boundaries of an Arab Palestine have yet to be determined by
consensus and negotiation. Officially, the PLO is committed to the goal of a secular Palestine to replace all of
Israel, a Palestine in which Jew, Moslem, and Christian
would have equal status. At the same time that more extreme
groups insist that only an Arab dominated Palestine is acceptable, others, perhaps a majority, consider the territories
of the West and East Banks and perhaps South Lebanon
would provide a sufficient territorial base for the establishment of a Palestinian state. More and more, this demand is
being expressed politically to Arab governments and to
world powers. Behind this thrust lies the threat of disruption, of terror, of embargo, and of war.

We began this chapter with quotations from interviews
during what we have termed the sense of nationalistic
peoplehood that illustrate the condition of narcissistic rage.
Later interviews demonstrated a considerable recovery of
self-esteem and transformation of rage to acts of aggression.
Paradoxically, terrorist and military success and the attention
these engendered actually reduced the quantity of rage, although none of its ostensible causes were altered. Identity
with a hoped for Palestine nation became a source of
personal—although often bitter—pride; grandiose self-
images were constructed and, under the impact of reality,
gradually modified. While radical factions could still attract
persons in the state of chronic narcissistic rage and could
sometimes mount suicide missions against Israeli citizens, the
majority of activists were more gratified by the sense of
belonging to increasingly organized national forces.

The October War of 1973 provided Palestinian forces the
opportunity for conventional military engagement alongside

those of established Arab states. Thereafter, vast resources of Palestinian energy were directed to the formation of a national political structure, involving constant internal negotiation and consensus building and external diplomacy in the search for recognition. Many Middle-East historians and political analysts have observed that in recent years, evidence of a politically maturing and realistic self-regard have appeared, still fragile, perhaps, and subject to regression, but manifested in some movement toward increased political responsibility—including occasional condemnation of some terrorist actions. Self-esteem, once achieved, will seek reflection in favorable opinion of others without, of course, any diminution of the identity on which self-esteem depends. The hallmarks of narcissistic maturity, wisdom and empathy with others, may have begun to appear in some of the statements of leading spokesmen and in the assessments by individual Palestinian personalities.

Youssef's struggle against rage

We will now report a single case history in order to provide a glimpse of the progressive development of self-involvement with the idea of the nation, and of the personal struggles that are entailed for individuals caught in the conflict of their people. Such longitudinal studies are, of course, basic tools of psychiatric understanding of individual motivation and behavior. In this case, as with most Palestinians, the involvement of self with national identity did not need emphasis as it represents central issues in the personality function. Youssef's experience is reported here, not because it is typical of a Palestinian youth, but because of his sensitivity and eloquence. Furthermore, his experience illustrates the intense struggle against narcissistic regression and rage that he waged in complete consciousness. At the same time, there is no major element in his life experience and personal struggle that is not widely represented in the youth—and others as well—of the Palestinian people.

Youssef is a college teacher in the sciences in his early thirties; he has been in the United States for two years. Of middle height and solid proportions, he habitually declares his Arab identity with his clothing, a Moroccan rain-cape, for example. He has an imposing presence, yet he is soft spoken and gentle in manner. He exudes a quality of thoughtfulness and integrity that is impressive to his students, as is the obvious pain expressed in his gaze when he talks about Jerusalem, the center of his dreams.

Youssef was born in the Christian Quarter of Jerusalem near the Jaffa Gate, the youngest of six children and the only one to gain a higher education and to leave the Middle East. His father was a small shopkeeper.

"The first thing I remember in my life is the streets of Jerusalem and feeling frightened by them but safe because my family was with me. The war (of 1948) came when I was seven. I remember soldiers running in the streets, the curfew. My family was afraid of Jewish terrorists. Bombs exploded, but I felt safe with my family. One night I woke up in the arms of my mother who was running and carrying me to safety from an attack on our area."

The family made its exodus to Bethlehem and lived with an uncle for the next year. Youssef missed the sights and sounds and crowds of Jerusalem. After a year, his family succeeded through connections with relatives in placing him in a French Missionary College in Jerusalem; his talent for mathematics was soon recognized and entry to a British High School was followed by a scholarship at the University at Florence where he studied for four years, contributing to his support—and his family's—by tutoring. His family objected to his failure to follow tradition. "Why leave Jerusalem, it is the center of the world." While he insisted on his personal independence he felt the pull. "Every summer when I came

back, I would see Jerusalem with entirely new eyes. The
rooms of my house became smaller every time I visited but
each time I came to love it more—Jerusalem came to have a
new meaning. First the meaning was of timelessness, more
and more. Then, I realized Jerusalem is both time and space,
and as one grows it becomes more time and less space. It is a
state of mind and particularly belongs to its inhabitants,
whoever they may be, whatever religion, and through them
to the world, but *first* to them."

At 23 years of age, Youssef began to teach in a college on
the West Bank; his students were refugees. "I was slow in
developing political consciousness; I was committed to ideas
of reconciliation. I was religious. When I taught refugees I
saw that mine was a luxury position—I just hadn't suffered as
they had. My anger grew. Exile is a terrible condition, but not
just the cold and the hunger. It is a condition of being in a
place that is not my country, in a society not of my culture, of
living in the enemy's camp. It is the experience of being
bombarded every day by a foreign way of seeing one's self
and one's homeland—it destroys one's person, one's identity." The turning point came when Israel attacked the Jordanian village of Es-Samur in 1966 and obliterated the
homes there—"that is a terrible, inhuman thing to do to
human beings." He feared being forced to join the Jordanian
Army, as many Palestinians were at that time—"but who wants
to join the army of Hussein; they call us Palestinians 'Arab
dirt'! The outrage made me conscious of my position of
being a Palestinian, of having no justice of my own to appeal
to. I remembered the teachings of my father when I was a
child; he taught me what it had been like under the Turks,
then under the British, then under the Jordanians. He said
that I would learn what it was like to be a subjugated person
when I grew up. Finally, I couldn't tolerate the feeling of
being a third class citizen under Hussein—I am at least a

person." He left Jordan for Lebanon; he carried his Palestinian identity with him.

In Beirut, Youssef found himself feeling more and more
an exile and felt that the condition was forced on him. "My
visa was temporary, the police watched all of us, some they
provoked and deported. They were afraid of us and we were
afraid of them. I could not go home to Jerusalem under
foreign rule and I could not have a home anywhere." The
June War of 1967 completed the sense of exile, finally releas-
ing long-avoided anger and finally confirming Youssef's
Palestinian identity in contrast to the cosmopolitan status that
he had striven to attain. "When I heard the announcement of
the fall of Jerusalem on the radio, I was stunned. I ran
through the streets. I tried to call my family but for four
months I could not reach them. For months my Palestinian
friends—then I had no other friends—and I would sit and
talk, sometimes weep. We would remember small details of
life in Jerusalem, wondering what had happened to the
milkman, for instance. Sometimes we would burst into wild,
hysterical laughter. I dreamed many times a nightmare: I
would be alone in the streets of Jerusalem, the curfew would
be in force, I would hear footsteps of Israeli soldiers behind
me. I would run, they would shoot, I would feel blood running down my back. But I knew that I would escape because
they were my streets, it was my territory. Sometimes I would
see my mother's face covered with blood." Youssef recalls his
agony as he would wait for the posting of the lists every day
of those who had lived and those who had died in the war.

"I saw a photograph then of the Mosque of Omar with an
Israeli soldier standing in front. I couldn't grasp it. It was
incomprehensible. I felt anger, rage, bitterness, loss. I saw an
elderly Palestinian man beside the road and I burst out in
rage at him. He said, 'Calm down young man; the Crusaders
were here for three hundred years, these people have been

here only nineteen'." Again, as at many points in his struggle, Youssef utilized this remark to regain perspective. "I realized that Jerusalem was not just a place, but place and time combined to represent an ultimate, humane meaning."

Youssef became disconsolate; his visa had expired and he was refused a renewal as the Lebanese put pressure on Palestinians; he went into hiding, going from town to town and friend to friend. His money ran out but he was unable to teach or even to think clearly due to his preoccupation with the fall of Jerusalem and concern for his family. His escape from this state grew, he thinks, from the extraordinary kindness of the owner of a shabby little restaurant who spontaneously gave him meals. This kindness led Youssef to resume his teaching as a means of passing on something of himself to others. His students were Palestine refugees and he felt their "hopeless situation—they were oppressed, they had no positive sense of identity and no hope for the future; no hope, that is, for something to be proud of in themselves and in their community. They needed to end their sense of inferiority, the feeling that they had been made the sacrificial lamb of the world's mistakes."

"It is the core of tragedy that people only started thinking about Palestinians with the outbreak of Palestinian violence." As the hijackings and terrorist attacks of 1968 drew attention to the Palestinians, Youssef found that he could not sustain his life-long condemnation of all human violence. He began to feel that violence against oppression is sometimes morally justified. "The Palestinians have a proverb 'He who takes the blows is not the one who counts them.' I read Fanon and I agree with him: being in exile is in itself a kind of violence; being in refugee camps is even worse—personal, direct, oppressive violence. Some Palestinians became paranoid, developed terrible personal problems. Some solved their dilemma by becoming super-Arabs or super-Americans; racists—that's even worse." Youssef came to believe that

there was no other way for a people threatened with
obliteration—that sooner or later they must fight back and
the only possible way involved assertion; the only possible
assertion was violence even though such action required willingness to give one's life.

Luckily for himself, Youssef personally was able to choose
against violent actions but he regards this as a luxury. "If a
man must give his life to be a man and to have a Palestine,
that is to be accepted and mourned—even honored. I can
give my life to my Palestinianness but not my death. I can
give my life through my work, my teaching, my personal
example in living and by declaring that I am Palestinian but I
cannot criticize my brothers who give their deaths for their
nation." He gradually became able to do research and teach
again. "Teaching is communication and when I couldn't
communicate with myself—that part of myself which is
Jerusalem that was torn out of me—I couldn't teach. I found
that although I am exiled I have Jerusalem with me eternally
in my heart; I found that one could go forward to Palestine.
My people are not living in myths any more. They have
decided to find a new way and go forward; that is why they
have formed action groups."

Youssef came to the United States in 1972, assisted by
officials who respected his qualities as an intellectual and as a
person. He has completed further studies and teaches in a
college. He quietly asserts his Palestinian identity when he
meets with Americans and often talks with American Jews. "I
feel that I am a metaphysical Jew, that I can never forget
Jerusalem. Every year we send greetings and write, as did the
Jews, 'Next year in Jerusalem' and I believe that someday I
can return to Jerusalem, when it belongs to its people, when
geography is humanized. Then, too, Jerusalem will belong to
all peoples."

The foregoing comments were all made in 1973; by 1975
Youssef's sense of "national self" had undergone still further

consolidation and the previous sense of humiliation had been transformed into some degree of pride. "My Palestinianness was defined by others before and I resent that. The FBI would interview me when there were attacks on Europe. Why? When I travel they insist that I am Palestinian. It is a situation that forces me to Palestinian consciousness." But Youssef responded to this definition from outside by a personal redefinition. "I decided, a lot of us decided, to define ourselves. It goes on in many places, free discussions. Not about what others say we are—refugees, or people without rights, or terrorists—but what we really are and want to be, human beings, a people, people with ordinary human rights, even if we have to fight for them. You know, our leadership is one of the most democratic in the world, much more democratic than any of the Arab States. Palestine is alive today; Jerusalem is alive today. I have more perspective on the meaning of being Palestinian. My mother used to point out the red poppies on the hills outside of Jerusalem in the spring—she called them the blood of Jesus; I have learned that long ago they were called the blood of Adonis—life returns."

The 1973 War did not affect Youssef deeply. "At first, all I felt was that it was a little game that could be used for politics. I couldn't understand the excitement of my Arab friends but I saw that they needed to have pride. We already had pride in being ourselves and the War didn't make much difference, although we were glad that Palestinian troops stood very strong on Golan."

In 1974 Youssef returned to Lebanon to help develop some new Arabic texts in his field. He spent many days in refugee camps talking with children who would be using his books but also talking with adults; hearing over and over the detailed stories of family displacement and tragedy—daily he would return in tears. But he found hope, too. "Every youth in the camps, women as well as men, has a new consciousness.

The bible of Palestinian youth is Frantz Fanon; drawing from it they reject definitions given them by the West and they say 'We will define ourselves'." Violence, in Youssef's new view, is necessary to resist the imposition of humiliating conditions. He noted with respect that even he required an escort into the camps, that violence in defense of the privacy of camp territory was only to be expected.

There have been some shifts in attitude in the past two years; Youssef now is equally unforgiving of Israel and of oppressive Arabs—the Hussein regime of Jordan and the Saudis. These he regards as following imperialist lines, as depriving their own people as well as Palestinians of freedom to define themselves, of an essential human dignity. "There was a poster in the Camp near Beirut; it showed the North Vietnamese soldier handing a flag to the people of the Portuguese colonies of Africa." Youssef feels that there will have to be a Palestine State, although he is not enthusiastic about the prospect; "it may distract people from the real struggle." Standing up to oppression, countering violence to the masses with counter violence, gaining a place in the world and in history, going forward to Palestine; these are all elements in Youssef's stance. He works to these ends, very hard indeed. He writes and edits and speaks, helping to bring order and articulation to the Palestinian cause which is his. His rage has dissipated into purposefulness; someday, he believes, he will walk in his own city, Jerusalem, as a free man.

Some dynamics of Youssef's self-involvement with Palestine

One of the reasons for choosing to sketch some of Youssef's development in relation to his people is that his personal self development has been unusually felicitous. As the youngest son, he was unquestionably the apple of his mother's eye; we note that at the age of seven he recalls feeling personally secure in the midst of war—secure in his family's bosom. His considerable talent was recognized early, first by his family and then by his teachers. It has continued to develop until it has been recognized as it is today. He is gifted and appreciated. Unlike many Palestinian families, his own remained intact and functional; despite inconveniences it was economically comfortable until he was 25 years old, when the 1967 War finally intruded and displaced the family from Jerusalem. Youssef's personal self-esteem has always been high; he is respected and liked to the point of having charisma.

Obviously, it would have been possible to describe the vicissitudes of more typical Palestinian youth who experienced refugeeism or internal exile and whose narcissistic development was impinged on by familial disruption from physical and status displacement, as was true for most of the subjects whose comments were reported in the opening section of this chapter. However, the very integrity of Youssef's personal self development provides an opportunity to make observations of the impact of disruptions of the primary group of the Palestinian people on the narcissistic balance of the extended self, and we will confine our comments to this dynamic.

Youssef was inculcated with the attitudes of subject peoplehood by his father and uncles who instructed him, somewhat bitterly, in the art of living under foreign domination—an instruction which he ultimately rejected but which was useful in curbing a reaction of humiliated rage to the Israeli occupation of Jerusalem when the old man reminded him of the virtues of resignation. This, of course, finally failed as a defense measure and was replaced by a complex mixture of "moral" rationalization, action by helping others—unfortunate refugees—and political activity. He regards this as a burdensome but inescapable mission.

Almost the first element of Youssef's awareness of self-

extension was to the concrete locus of Jerusalem; at seven,
when the family was in Bethlehem, he "missed Jerusalem."
During his student days abroad, the home site became more
and more important, although he made valiant efforts to
free himself of this attachment by converting the feeling for
a concrete place into an abstract—and more portable—set of
feelings. He was tempted to give up his Palestinian identity
and even argued with his family against such inconvenient
localism; his thought was to become a "free" human being
and to carry with him only the abstract human and moral
meaning of his homeplace. However, metaphysics proved
to be no substitute for geography, and rootless cosmo-
politanism was no consolation for the extension of the self
invested in the place to which he belonged and which belonged to him.

As Youssef remarked, "my political consciousness was late
in coming"; the struggle between personal self development
and the pull of components of extended self occupied much
of his narcissistic energy for, unlike most of his compatriots,
Youssef had a genuine choice; he could, in practical terms,
have escaped from exile identity. In fact he refused to identify himself with Palestine but regarded himself as Jerusalem-
ite as long as he could sustain that position. However, for
Youssef, the core of the geographic self investment was extremely powerful and inescapable; struggle and delay as he
might it seemed almost inevitable that this should expand to
encompass the Palestinian people and, eventually, the sense
of Palestinian national identity as part of his extended self.

Political consciousness began almost immediately when
Youssef began working with refugee Palestinians. A main
component of this was indignation, a precursor of rage. He
observed the shameful hopelessness of refugee students and
their impotence to change their situations. He heard their
stories over and over, stories of forcible disinheritance. He
identified with them and became angered and indignant;

immediately he began to seek political solutions as he does to this day. And as he did so, he became immediately involved in the wider Palestinian cause. Paradoxically, he tended to feel that Israel could be approached by rational argument and appeal. Some of his teachers had been Jews and he was intellectually in tune with the universalistic stream of Jewish philosophy, and opposed violence toward Israel. However, immediately before his eyes was the humiliating treatment of Palestinians by Jordanians and other Arabs. This made him extremely angry and finally led to his leaving Jerusalem rather than submit to insult; he continued to have this feeling in Lebanon, however. Open outrage followed soon, this time directed at Israel, following the destruction of Es-Samur. Both his sense of national identity and of outrage were fully mobilized. For the first time, Youssef was committedly Palestinian.

Youssef's response to the capture of Jerusalem by Israel in 1967 speaks for itself. He reports he felt that "Jerusalem was torn out of me." One could scarcely describe a narcissistic wound more poignantly; the sense of self was itself mutilated. His recurrent dream contains the curious mixture of a sense of triumph "because it's my territory," and injury— here the wounds to Jerusalem become those of his own body. His reaction was a mixture of sorrow, humiliation and rage. He felt personally devastated and for a year and a half was unable to work as he carried on a fierce internal struggle at a number of levels, principally between violent rage and an extraordinary commitment to self-control, reason and metaphysical universalism, but also between personal-self and group loyalties, between attitudes of enculturated dependent subjecthood and radical rebelliousness (some of this had been foreshadowed in his adolescent revolt against family strictures), and between fragmentation and coherence of his personality.

Youssef was and is a personality of considerable resources; he observed a number of instances of radical solution to plights similar to his. He had friends who succumbed to suicidal rage and died in almost futile acts of violence against either Israel's borders or Arab police; some retreated into hopelessness and sank into refugee despair; quite a few seemed to escape the Palestinian identity altogether—at least for the moment—and integrated into other societies. Youssef resolved his own woundedness in large part by empathic merger with the Palestinian people; he found an outlet from helplessness by helping his people. At the same time he acknowledged that he was inescapably bound up with his "Palestinianness." Much as he disapproved of violence and regarded acts of terror as tragic, he nevertheless found grim satisfaction in the attention that these actions brought.

Later he was to be less ambivalently proud of Palestinian performance in conventional battle. This mirroring attention by powerful outsiders and by Israel not only reduced the sense of humiliation but contributed to the shift to active espousal of the Palestinian cause. In fact, only when this healing by merger had taken place did Youssef find a return of his creative and active capacities and become able to resume his career—always thereafter devoting a portion of creative activity to the Palestinian cause. He had, in his personal life, passed through a stage of narcissistic rage and developed an identity as a Palestinian nationalist.

When Youssef says in 1975 that he will someday walk in Jerusalem as a free man, he is not only speaking metaphorically. For he is now deeply committed to the purpose of full Palestinian rights in traditional Palestinian territory. Although he was less than fully candid with his interviewer on this subject, he strongly hinted that this goal could be achieved only by a massive revolutionary revision of the character of the regimes of the Middle East, both of Arab states and of Israel. The struggle of his people as he now sees it is not between them and the Israeli state but between human dignity and oppressive systems. He has no quarrels with Jews nor any wish for their displacement as a people, but he has deep hostility to the Jewish state. Revealingly, when he reviewed the foregoing notes, he urged consideration of two major views; first, that we should note that the fierce-sounding statements about "drinking Jewish blood" or driving "Jews into the sea" should be understood as ancient Arabic metaphors expressing displeasure but not intent. "We Arabs speak to one another that way because it is classical but not because we intend to harm the other," and second, he urged awareness of the deep resentment of the position of Palestine Arabs in Israel, especially by those living in that state: "Of course, they will not tell you or the Jews, but with us they talk differently when they are very certain that we understand; it is not by accident that two of the main PLO intellectuals graduated from the Hebrew University."

Youssef's recovery of self-coherence has been accomplished; he has integrated his Palestinian nationalist identity into his larger sense of self. His work is productive and widely respected; he is confident of himself and of his purposes, although he recognizes the great difficulty of achieving the latter. This level of narcissistic maturation has been consolidated by activity—helping refugees and working for his cause; by recognition—he is proud of the attention commanded by Palestine and by the search for dignity; and by purpose—narrowly, the humane liberation of Palestine, broadly, the liberation of "humanity from oppression"—and he presses vigorously for the realization of those ideals. Youssef and people like him will work out their own destinies in their transactions with each other and the world they live in; we would only hope that the enduring quality of the self-system will not be underestimated in the inevitable processes of political accommodation in the Middle East.

Stages of Palestinian political-self development

Using Youssef's experience of an emerging extended-self structure in relation to Arab Palestine as the dominant primary group extension, we are now in a position to outline a

Political and Extended-Self Model Development

Stage of Political Self-Awareness	Political Object Relations	Extended-Self Configuration
I. Subject people-hood —1917	Subjugated family-clan as primary group.	Coherence and balance within subject status.
II. Sense of people-hood c. 1917–1954	Rebellion vs. dependency, coherence vs. outsiders. Share conspicuous defeat and disinheritance.	Assertion of autonomy followed by massive trauma, shame, regression and withdrawal.
III. Sense of nationalistic peoplehood c. 1954–1968	Incoherence. Shared outrage but community in vengeance. Turn toward violent action vs. enemy.	Fragmentation, humiliation. Narcissistic rage with archaic grandiosity.
IV. Perception of nationhood c. 1968–1974	Nation as object. Struggle for political coherence. Directed action-aggression.	Merger with extended grandiose self (nation) and idealized self-object. Demands for mirroring.
V. Movement toward national statehood 1974—	Demand for autonomy and political parity. Political organization—some action by more realistic methods.	Internalization of national self-object by merger and organized action; extended-self esteem from recognition of nation by outsiders.

general model of narcissistic extended self development of the Palestinian people in the form that we realize is both simplified and idealized but which we regard as representing modal normative configurations. As has been outlined earlier, there was some lag time between the shock of forcible disinheritance in 1948 and the rallying to a sense of Palestinian national identity, which most observers now date around 1954.

The first two stages of this model of political and extended-self development have been reconstructed from the reports of Youssef and others who, like him, were initially exposed to traditional family and culture patterns. We began this chapter with fragments of interviews reflecting individuals' sense of nationalistic peoplehood and the accompanying self experiences of narcissistic rage and will now report on observations from succeeding stages of political and concomitant self development. Before proceeding, however, we would like to emphasize that the emergence and evolution of the extended self is a process in which each succeeding stage retains elements of preceding stages of development which are often manifested in times of stress. Our descriptive model represents the dominant emerging themes and postulated dynamics of each stage.

Merger, mirroring and the sense of nationhood

"Who does *SHE* think *SHE* is to say we don't exist, that we never existed, that there was never a Palestinian entity? We will show her; *SHE* will see that we exist! We were there, it was our home long before *SHE* ever touched our earth. Now we will fight—*SHE* will see. Who is *SHE*? That woman has no name; for us *SHE* does not exist. Well, I exist and I'm proud to be a Palestinian; we are an old people but we are becoming a new people. For too long we looked to others to help us out, we listened to their promises; now we look to nobody but ourselves. The world knows we exist since our soldiers destroyed those planes that flew to our territory occupied by the enemy. And they will know it more, more and more." The year was 1969. "*SHE*" referred to Israel's Prime Minister, whom the young chemist in Boston refused to name. He was one of a group of eight or ten young men who met regularly to discuss developments in the Middle East and their hopes and plans for Palestine, as well as their own plans for action to "explain" the reality of Palestine to Americans. Sometimes they called themselves a "Palestine cell" and they were proud of it.

Actually, only a year before the young chemist made this statement he had lapsed into an attitude of persistent embitterment in relation to his sense of nationality, even as he had become increasingly successful in his career in industry. He felt himself to be a hopeless exile, reduced to impotent expressions of anger and hurt which, it seemed, nobody would listen to except his fellow exiles. His position was passive. He unhappily accepted his fate. Several events precipitated his shift to activity and optimism. "I have to admit that I'd almost given up; I didn't want any one to notice that I was a Palestinian, not even an Arab. I wanted to be myself, a person, a chemist, to be left alone. But it felt bad to be ashamed all the time. I thought of going to Syria to work in my uncle's pharmacy; at least I'd be somebody there. I have to admit that Karameh (March, 1968) and the hijackings made a big difference; some people began to ask about us. Even when they attacked our methods, they at least admitted that Palestinians existed. I believe in fighting. If you are oppressed and there is no justice and no one will listen and they say, 'Who are the Palestinians?,' then you have to fight. I myself am not a physical fighter, not a hijacker—I thought of joining the commandos, but that's silly for me. But I can fight *my* way. I can explain who we Palestinians are and why some of our commandos are fighting; I'm glad for their actions."

The young chemist began to get together with fellow Palestinians, not just for sociability but to plan strategies and discuss future possibilities. Together with other groups, they pressed for public debates; they were both outraged and delighted when a public presentation of the Palestinian case at a local university was cancelled because of bomb threats by radical Zionists. As the "Palestinian cell" continued its meetings the content of discussion changed from shared sorrow and rage to shared satisfaction in commando exploits and to excited discussions about the future of Palestine, discussions increasingly fueled by the rather sudden appearance of a literature; leaflets and pamphlets designed to explain the problems of the Middle East through Palestinian eyes. The young chemist and his friends distributed this material personally and began to attend larger meetings and discussion groups. During the twenty months of casual dialogue with the young chemist and his friends, into 1970, they developed a formidable array of ideological argument, centering around varieties of formulation of armed popular and political struggle with the aim of establishing "a democratic, nonsectarian state of Palestine, within which Jew, Moslem, and Christian would enjoy political equality." The degree to which the struggle would need to be conducted in Jordan and Lebanon as well as within Israel was subject to much debate. There was little talk of class warfare; rather, the adversary was seen as imperialism. There was virtually none of the fire-eating talk of the previous period about expelling Jews; rather, the question was one of transforming Palestinian society. Their ideological developments were invariably based on an assumption of Palestinian autonomy that often seemed unreal and grandiose as they proposed political acquiescence by other states and peoples in transformative processes.

Between 1968 and 1970, the young chemist was transformed. He had passed from a state of helpless rage to demoralization, and, during the period of discussion, from demoralization into a self-confident assertion of national identity and active effort to recruit recognition and understanding of the Palestinian position. He had passed from a position of petulant complaint that he and his people were treated unjustly to one of believing that they must create their own justice by their own actions and, however ambiguous the ideas, to the view that the Palestinians would somehow extend justice to other peoples in Palestine and the Arab world. He had acquired a language for the concept of political action and even modest skills in argument. He was personally changed too, less sour and discouraged and, it may be added, more contented in his social life.

A somewhat similar process took place among the youth of Palestine in many other places as well. A young Palestinian from Damascus said in 1970, "I'm a commando. I've had good training, eight weeks in the desert. I didn't have to do that, I wanted to! Sure, I could study in England or America, but I want to stay here. I'm on call and I'm ready to go and fight when they activate my unit. Why? Because we must; no one will respect us until we show that we can fight for our country, until we show that we deserve our country. It's a matter of self respect, as simple as that." He walked with a bit of swagger; his confidence in himself and his identity as a Palestinian was, at age 20, well established. His training was for a regular unit of Fatah Commando. He would undergo further training next year, meanwhile meeting monthly for instruction.

Again in Rama, in 1970, ten years after we had heard bitter complaints and the comparison to "caged birds," a student at home from the Hebrew University for a visit was eager to display his pride and confidence in being a Palestinian; "Of course, I'm a Palestinian Arab. My citizenship is in Israel but my people, my nation, is Palestine. That doesn't make me an enemy of the state, even though I want to

change it. They understand that now. Before, if an Arab
criticized policies he was treated as an enemy and sometimes
bad things were done. But it's much better now. There are
Arab members of the Knesset and they say what they want to.
They criticize the mistreatment of Arab citizens. Either we
are citizens and have full rights, or we're not citizens at all.
We have to stand up for our rights in this country and I will.
There are many injustices for us, but we can talk about them;
we can demand justice for ourselves. It is different for Palestinians in the occupied territories or for those in exile. They
have to fight in different ways and we respect that. But we
cannot, we don't want to fight that way, with armies and
terror. The way we fight is in Israel; we fight politically, we
demand recognition and justice for all Palestinians; their
right to return, our right to full citizenship, the right of all of
us, Jew, Christian and Moslem, to an equal voice in the
Palestine state. I think it can come about with the pressure
from the outside because the government must treat us more
fairly to avoid pressure from the inside. Partly, it is our
mission within Israel to show the government and the rest of
the world that we Palestinians are good citizens if we are
treated fairly, if we are treated like citizens. We cannot do
that with war and terror but by speaking out and voting and
by obeying even the laws that we want to change. In the long
run we will never accept a Jewish state but we will accept the
Jewish people in Palestine as citizens just like us."

This young man demonstrated the circumspection that has
come to characterize the Palestine Arab inhabitants of Israel.
His statements appear to combine caution in dealing with
outsiders who might, indeed, represent the internal police of
the government, and the aspiration for a changed status that
was pressed only to an acceptable limit. The interviewers had
no doubt but that they were encountering an extremely
skillful spokesman who almost certainly harbored private
sentiments of a more strident nationalism than were ex-

pressed; nevertheless, the degree of pride and confidence in the possibility of a Palestinian nation was clearly evident. Rather than appealing to the interviewer to accept the validity of a complaint, the young man asserted his claims for justice and his own determination to press those claims. He was obviously gratified by the recognition that Palestinians had achieved and perhaps unrealistically certain of the eventual outcome of Palestinian actions which he saw as the establishment of a secular democratic state of Palestine.

By no means were all Arabs in Israel or in the occupied areas so confident. Many seemed in conflict, simultaneously expressing both bitterness and begrudging respect toward Israel and Israelis while asserting their Arab identity. In Jerusalem in 1972 we frequently heard comments such as: "Those Kibbutz people, they think they are supermen. They come here and march through our streets as though they owned them. They don't like to pay for what they buy. The government made propaganda that we charge twice what we expect to get so they demand we give them things for half the price. That's humiliating and it forces us to act like cheats to keep our business. Then they accuse us of what they've forced us to do; actually it's what they do themselves." In point of fact, the shopkeepers and taxi-drivers of the old city were far from subservient. Frequently they took advantage of opportunities to confront Israeli visitors and shoppers with level-eyed contempt at some outrageous offer or by holding to the right-of-way to make clear that the territory was, for them perhaps, more than equally their own.

During this period, between 1967 and 1973, a number of efforts were made to develop and sustain interchanges between Palestinian Arabs and Israelis by both international and Israeli-sponsored organizations, for purposes of increasing understanding and reconciling inter-communal differences. We have reviewed several of these experiments in Jerusalem, the Hebrew University, and the West Bank and can report that none, to our knowledge, resulted in a community of purpose or relationship of significant duration. Participants from both sides were subjected to the pressures and pull of primary loyalty to their distinct sense of national identity and this almost invariably proved more powerful than the attractions of inter-group relationships. It appears to us that the boundaries of national identity were being established and defined, especially for the Palestine Arabs, and that in these circumstances a profound segregation of relationships was psychologically necessary and socially enforced. The best working relations—and there were many such—appeared to develop where the element of national identity was thoroughly established, as between village officials and occupation authorities. Meanwhile, these levels of contact within Israel and the occupied territories contributed to a considerable revision of the stereotypes held of each side by the other, a revision which was rapidly transmitted to Palestinians in exile.

The movement toward the perception of Palestinian nationhood achieved its psychological goal of visibility and acknowledgment largely through acts of violence that forced Israel to take Palestinians seriously. Whatever official stands were taken by Palestinian leaders, the terrorist activities between 1968 and 1972 were almost universally sanctioned, even by Palestinians who opposed violent methods personally, as did Youssef. During that period, none of the many subjects who were interviewed failed to express some personal sense of satisfaction that, as several remarked, "at least now they know Palestine exists." Typical was a young man in Jerusalem who said, "I'm a quiet man and I just want to do my work. I don't believe in violence. But I notice now that when I travel people who see my passport or learn that I am a Palestinian treat me with respect—maybe they're a little afraid. I'm ashamed to admit it, but when I look back I realize that I was suffering all the time from feeling anonymous, apologetic and a little ashamed. Everyone needs respect. The hijackings and even the Olympic Village attack have changed that, and even when I disapprove I have to admit that I benefit personally and I can't condemn the actions, at least not among my friends. The funny thing is that I used to see the doctor all the time for my stomach and because I worried about my heart, and now I feel quite well." Clearly, neurotic self-concern was relieved by increased self-esteem derived from identification with his people.

Not only was there satisfaction with the ending of the pain of narcissistic disacknowledgment as well as with the mirroring of existence in the eyes of others, but there was a consolidation of identity, a sense of merger of the individual self with the perception of nationhood. The nation was often seen in grandiose terms, "You will see, the whole world will see what Palestinians are. No one knows yet that we are the most modern Arabs. Our girls are liberated—some of them are commandos. Our people are educated and we have technical experts in almost everything; the rest of the Arabs depend on Palestinians for this. We are democratic and do not believe in false kings and sheikhs. We have much more military power than anyone knows about. To the world we may look like refugees, but when we are ready we will strike; then you will know." It appears to us that such heady national grandiosity, arising out of the beginnings of recovery from shattered self-esteem contributed considerably to the defiant behavior of some Palestinian elements in Jordan in 1970, and to miscalculated coup plans that precipitated the battles and repression of "Black September." While Palestinians were openly expressing their feelings, the Palestinian movement lacked organizational ability to direct and control its own forces.

Paradoxically, the defeat of Black September appears to have reinforced and confirmed this independent Palestinian identity. Not only did King Hussein's regime administer a serious set-back to Palestinian aspirations, but both Syria and Iraq rapidly retreated from their gestures of military support, and even Egypt's Nasser, who died the day after he had mediated a cease fire, had been less than vigorous in giving his political blessings. Palestine finally knew that it would have to stand on its own feet and Palestinians were almost bitterly pleased. One leader articulated his feeling, "It used to be that 'only Arab unity can liberate Palestine'; now it is that 'only Palestine can bring about Arab unity.' Our dependence is ended. We used to think that we could manipulate the Arab states and they would help us with our battles. Now we think of them only as allies; they will have to deal with us as equals. We know now that we must organize our whole nation and that it will take a long time. But it feels real, it's not just an idea, it doesn't depend on others. Even though we are worse off, our base in Jordan shattered, our people scattered, many of them under occupation, we have more confidence because it is real, it depends on us. We aren't dreamers anymore."

The new sense of realism was almost immediately manifested in the willingness on the part of many Palestinians to consider that the "dream" of return to the whole Palestine would have to be deferred, at least until the achievement of independent statehood. Here the internal discussion among fellow Palestinians and dialogue with outsiders such as the interviewers assumed a decided difference. In fact, scarcely any phenomenon was more impressive to an interviewer with long acquaintance with Palestinian people than the sense of being shut out of personal confidence with respect to internal political thinking. Between 1972 and 1975 a number of subjects would maintain the official stance that the only acceptable political aim was the establishment of a secular democratic state in the place of Israel (we are not here reporting on more radical ideological variations), and would avoid discussing any alternatives except for mild hints that "we really don't talk about these matters with outsiders." These subjects had not only achieved identity with the Palestine nation but had incorporated the sense of exclusiveness into their own encounters; the personal self began to reflect the extended national self boundaries.

Some Palestinians who were interviewed were exceptions to the general attitude of national exclusiveness. One middle-aged leader had actually published an argument for a West Bank-Gaza territorial state, "Yes, to tell the truth I feel threatened, actually I've received threats by mail and phone. I don't know from where. But I have decided that my life does not mean that much as a stateless person. Actually, it's half of a life. So you see, I'm not making a foolish bargain. I am risking a half life which is sometimes worse than none in order to have a chance for a full life. When I say that Palestinians must admit the reality of Israel and, for the present at least, must form our own state on land that the whole world agrees belongs to us by right—it is even less than the U.N. Partition plan—I know it is a personal risk. The truth is, though, that many Palestinians agree with me and someone has to speak out. I don't think anything will happen to me because that would be bad as an example to the world but, you know, some of our people are crazy with frustration of their hopes and they think I'm a traitor. I guess my fate is in the hands of Allah, but it always is." A year later, 1975, the same man, still alive, had gone even further and entered into frank discussions with Israeli scholars in the United States. "I still get threats, but I feel safer now. The more that I talk with the other side, the more I feel Palestinian. It will take a few years for our people to discover that. Fatah doesn't approve officially, but when I talk with the leaders, they are at least interested and I know they discuss the plan themselves. They say that they must accommodate themselves to the radicals if they are to lead all the people. They don't expect the radicals, the ideologists or the political mercenaries to change but they think that most of their followers will accept the PLO position; they can be more realistic then. To tell the truth, I agree with them; you must be very strong and certain of yourself to change and it is as necessary for them to bring the people together around a plan they can accept as it is for me to take the next step. When they are ready, when they are strong enough, I think they will follow because it is realistic."

Movement toward national identity and feelings of parity

One of the more instructive observations of this study has been the rapidity and subtlety of shifts in narcissistic configuration of our subjects in their relations to their nation as well as the widespread generality of the changes. During the fifteen years since the close of the 1950s, we observed a shift from a sense of helplessness and narcissistic rage to a merger of personal and national identity in grandiose and idealized images. As this report is being formulated, that phase of narcissistic development appears to be in the process of transition. It is marked by a degree of re-internalization of important elements of the extended self. What was previously an object, the nation, is now increasingly a subject, part of the self. New objects, the outside world and especially Israel, the prime adversary, are acknowledged as existing. We have characterized this as a period of movement toward national identity. For at least some Palestinians an inner sense of psychological parity with nationals of Israel and the Arab states has been achieved.

In some individuals, the shifts in configuration of self are experienced as occurring quite suddenly. It is as though they remained in a stance such as that of narcissistic rage for prolonged periods while the preconditions for the next configuration are established. Once this has taken place, relatively small events appear to dissolve the previous state which crystallizes at a new level of organization. Consequently, past experience of an apparently stable equilibrium that includes political attitudes is an unreliable guide to current reality. Our subjects often reported, "After (a particular incident) I suddenly felt different." There is also a certain contagion of the process; after a few people, not necessarily important or influential, have provided a personal example and articulated the possibility of a new pathway for self-definition, others may follow. We have the impression, for example, that the onset of the stage of narcissistic rage occurred with dramatic suddenness some years following the trauma of displacement in 1948; for many individuals the experience relieved the state of hopelessness they were in, but the strikingly identical expression in places widely separated from each other suggests the diffusion of psychological invention to a receptive and prepared population. In any event, we often noted that the impressions of outside observers, including sometimes ourselves, were apt to be based on information concerning an earlier stage and this created a substantial impediment to understanding. Obviously, only current experience can provide a guide to responding with any effectiveness in encounters with a people undergoing such profound shifts in the organization of self. We are impelled to compare these changes with those observed in the course of intensive psychotherapy; we had really not expected to observe such important shifts in self-configuration occurring so widely and simultaneously in an entire people. (Similar shifts have been noted in Israel and among other Arab people, as described in other chapters of this report.)

We must add here that although the re-configurations that we have observed are widespread, they are not universal. We have not had the opportunity to interview members of the militant commando groups who espouse varieties of terrorism and/or radical revolutionary action in Arab states. But the reports of our subjects who know them, coupled with a review of their writings, suggest that in addition to their ideological differences they may have remained at levels of rage or grandiosity which have become institutionalized and ideologically rationalized in their political organizations. The leaders of these groups, such men as George Habash of the Popular Front for the Liberation of Palestine (PFLP), Ahmed Jabril of PFLP-General Command, or Nayif Hawatmah of the Popular Democratic Front for the Liberation of Palestine, are each quite extraordinary men of whom we think it likely that "private motives displaced on public objects and rationalized in terms of public interest"—in the classic formulation of power and personality of Lasswell—may be descriptive. However, this is a question beyond the scope of this report.[2] Whatever their drives for power or leadership or revolution may be, we assume that many of their followers are drawn to these groups by the opportunity to overcome narcissistic wounds through destructive action. Some of our subjects have known commandos who engaged in acts of terror and have expressed pity and sympathy for their state of being possessed by insatiable hatred, much like the description of Kamous in Fawaz Turki's *The Disinherited*.[3]

When Yasir Arafat spoke to the United Nations General Assembly in October 1974, posters were widely distributed in New York and other cities in the United States announcing "Palestine Lives," featuring the outlines of an abstract dove on a field of black, red and green (colors of the PLO flag), and "Palestine Forever," overprinted on a sea of Palestinian faces. This public assertiveness of movement toward national identity has been accompanied by the appearance of a greatly increased sense of self-esteem among at least some Palestinians.

The shift in attitude is less manifest in verbal statements than in behavior; our impression is that our subjects are acutely aware of feeling differently about their Palestinian-ness but that there is a lag in articulating the nature and dimensions of this feeling. In fact, this quality is one aspect of the changed attitude; rather than ventilating feelings about their perception of national identity—although personal ex-periences and feelings are easily elicited—there is a degree of restraint, of waiting, until a consensus is formed. In part, this attitude is the outcome of uncertainty about the international status of Palestinian questions in an era of intense maneu-vering and negotiation. This does not imply that political violence or war participation is psychologically improbable at this stage of self development. In fact, even the most confi-dent and hopeful subjects express strong feelings about that; feelings such as, "What is fundamental is that there must be a Palestinian state. We will resist attempts to impose a settle-ment on us. If there is no Palestinian state, there will be more fighting, more war." It seems clear that the basic issue for subjects such as these is the existence of a self-governing Palestine national entity on its own territory, though its boundaries would be psychologically negotiable. Injury to the extended self, that is, denial of the possibility of progress toward independent national identity, could represent a powerful stimulus to participation in violent conflict among subjects at this stage of self-configuration.

Another evidence of the changed attitude and sense of parity is the appearance, for the first time, of sustained discussions between Palestinians and Israelis in both Israel and the United States. In recent years, many task force groups with equal representation of Palestine Arab and Is-raeli scholars have been organized for the purpose of consid-ering specific regional problems. The assumption that underlies this new level of dialogue is that of planning for a future which could include an independent Palestinian na-tional entity. Such activity engenders sharp controversy, with respect either to the PLO or Israel, but the significant fact is that such discussions can be held at all, a phenomenon that was virtually unattainable, despite many efforts, prior to October 1973.

Data from the most recent phase that we have posited does not sustain any estimate as to its extent or consolidation. As this is written it is possible to say only that *some* Palestine Arab people appear to have attained internal cohesion and balance of extended self-esteem, combined with a sense of psychological boundaries. This attainment permits them to enter into encounters and transactions, even with adversaries, without apparent disturbance of self-esteem; indeed, they emerge with heightened confidence in their sense of national identity.

References

1. H. Kohut. "Thoughts on Narcissism and Narcissistic Rage," in THE PSYCHOANALYTIC STUDY OF THE CHILD, Vol. 27 (New York: Quadrangle Books, 1972), pp 360–400.
2. H. D. Lasswell. POWER AND PERSONALITY (New York: W. W. Norton, 1948).
3. F. Turki. THE DISINHERITED, 2nd ed (New York: Modern Reader, 1974), pp 170–174.

4

THE PEOPLE OF ISRAEL: THE DEFENSE OF LAND AND SELF

Israeli citizens have been interviewed by members of this committee between 1959 and 1975, the formal cut-off date of this investigation. Our notes have been reviewed in terms of the evidence of self-involvement of people with the land and state which we believe is so profound as to constitute a "narcissistic hypercathexis," that is, an identification of the self with the country which is of unusual depth and is totally involving for each individual citizen. We will permit the material to speak for itself to a large extent, adding comments on the dynamic patterns of reactivity of the self which affect the feelings, beliefs and attitudes of our subjects.

We will not undertake an extensive review of the long and important history of the Jewish people before the founding of the State in 1948, despite its profound dynamic significance to the people of Israel. It is, nevertheless, very real in the conscious and less-than-overt attitudes of Israelis. We have confined ourselves closely to living subjects whose words, we believe, demonstrate the impact of history in their lives, and the constant awareness of tradition and mission as part of their intimate selves. We have focused on modal configurations of shared self-involvement in the nation as these have manifested themselves in response to major events bearing on their state.

Jews have had a strongly developed sense of *peoplehood* for literally thousands of years, an awareness consolidated con-

stantly by long exile after 135 A.D. The idea of a homeland
and of a state never entirely disappeared and the *thrust for
statehood* emerged in organized form with the rise of Zionism
in the 1860's. The achievement of *statehood* in 1948 was
accompanied by intense investment of the self in the state by
virtually all Israeli citizens and by a great many Jews who
lived in other countries.

This sudden increase and spread of self-involvement focused on the necessity of coming to terms with the international "we" and "you" of the State and its neighbors. At each
major turn in these relationships, individual citizens responded as though the events, real or imagined, affected
them personally. Since the first issue was survival, which
could be pursued with unambivalent vigor, there was no
conflict of loyalties; this was followed by self-absorption in
nation-building. But the world did not leave Israel alone, nor
could Israelis avoid a painful sensitivity to the long history of
persecution and humiliation of the Jews in many countries.
Feelings of vulnerability, coupled with the intense need
never again to be humiliated, were intensified by continuing
Palestinian terrorist attacks. Israeli determination to elimi-
nate real and at times perhaps exaggerated threat, contributed to participation in the preemptive Sinai War of 1956
and continued to be an important factor in the June War of
1967, serving to overcome the *sense of national vulnerability*.
Following the successful prosecution of the June 1967 war,
there was a shared sense of expanded *autonomy*, a confidence
in the security of the state that sometimes reached unrealistic
proportions. This "splendid isolation" was shattered by Arab
state attacks initiating the October War of 1973. Israel's response was defensive, ill-prepared, and aggravated by a failure of Israeli intelligence. Injury to their self-esteem is still
evident in many. For some Israelis, the October War of 1973
led to another phase of self-development, a narcissistic maturation that enables acknowledgment of others. We shall

exemplify these developments from the experiences of our Israeli subjects.

Israel and the Israelis

"Israel is a land and a people." Jewish people have held sovereignty over the land of Israel three times in their thirty-five centuries of peoplehood which, according to tradition, began with the acceptance of the commandments of God by the patriarch, Abraham. The period of the first temple, for about 12 centuries until 586 B.C., is recorded in the Torah (Bible). Again, from 516 B.C. to 70 A.D., the period of the Second Temple, Jewish kingdoms flourished until they were overwhelmed by the Roman Empire—the last fortress, Masada, fell in 73 A.D. After centuries of outside rule and dispersal from the land, the Jewish people again achieved sovereignty over the land with the declaration of independence of Israel in 1948.

Some Jews always remained in the land of Israel, even under foreign occupation, although the number is estimated to have fallen as low as 10,000 at the turn of the nineteenth century when local conditions were anarchic and difficult. Far larger numbers were dispersed during the Diaspora to the outside world by a series of expulsions and massacres by the Roman and Byzantine Empires. In the Diaspora, Jews who held to their religion and peoplehood were persecuted by dominant religious and secular interests; they were massacred by Crusaders in Jerusalem in 1099, expelled from England in 1290 and from France in 1306. In Toledo, Spain, in 1355, 12,000 Jews were massacred by mobs; many were forcibly converted to Christianity in Spain in the 12th century and 180,000 were expelled from Spain in 1492. During the 18th and 19th centuries, hundreds of thousands of Jews were murdered in Russia and Poland; others from Russia were forced to resettle "in the Pale." This terrible story culminated in the most massive genocide in world history, the Holocaust murder of six million Jews by German Nazis and their European collaborators. Whatever accounts for the persecutions, the strength of Jewish peoplehood is undeniable.

Despite these troubles the Jews of the Diaspora have enjoyed long periods of peaceful community and have contributed much to the nations of which they were citizens. The qualities of respect for the Word and culture-based integrity placed Jewish individuals and subcommunities in special and valued positions again and again. Ironically, this was never more true than during the Golden Age of Islam when Jews, often having been expelled from Christian Europe, enjoyed positions of trust and value throughout the Moslem world— for centuries Jews were prominent as the physicians, philosophers, musicians, teachers, and advisors to sovereigns.

And in the Diaspora, the Jewish people contributed disproportionately to the common culture of humanity; to list the savants, the artists, the thinkers who have risen among the Jewish people is unnecessary. But the people had no territory, no state, and no sovereignty. Through the centuries many Jews found their heritage restrictive and austere, too dangerous sometimes, and many intermarried and assimilated and converted to the dominant faith of their place; some became secular cosmopolitans. Always, a substantial nucleus adhered to their heritage and raised their children by its tenets; they valued their peoplehood despite its great drawbacks.

Given these circumstances, it is not surprising that the advent of nationalism in Western civilization should immediately be reflected in the Jewish people. The idea of the return had long been celebrated among the people, and the phrase "Next year in Jerusalem" had been repeated for centuries. The Biblical oath was, "If I should forget thee, Oh Jerusalem, may my right hand forget its cunning!" Some sects kept the idea of a political return alive, but in the 1860's the idea of actual return to the land and revival of Jewish national life became widespread, independently arrived at in widely separated parts of the world. Jews in Israel began to construct a Jewish community in 1860 and this was followed by the founding of villages and schools and publishing efforts all dedicated to the return.

Meanwhile, in the Diaspora, the idea gained strength and the first "aliya" (immigration) from Europe began in 1881. By 1897 the first Zionist Congress was organized in Basle by a journalist, Theodor Herzl, and the World Zionist Organization was organized. As we have reported in Chapter 2, the Balfour Declaration was issued by the British Government in November, 1917, and a great power was thereby commited to recognition of aspirations for a national home for the Jewish people in Palestine. After this the Jewish community in Palestine received successive waves of immigration, mostly from Eastern Europe and after 1930 from Germany. The Jewish community organized political and, eventually, irregular military institutions; it founded school and social welfare systems, often in concert with the British Governor from whom the community won many concessions.

We have outlined the beginning of the Arab-Jewish conflict; from the Jewish point of view, Jewish communities were subject to terrorist attacks and engaged in measures to defend legally acquired land and rights. Attempts at partition by the British Government repeatedly failed as did the final attempt by the United Nations in 1948, largely because of Arab resistance to the idea. Meanwhile, the aliyas continued as refugees from Nazi terror arrived in the 1930's and most especially when the Second World War ended with hundreds of thousands of displaced vestiges of the European Jewish population in refugee status. When the State was proclaimed, an estimated 759,000 Jews and 126,000 non-Jews inhabited Israel's territory. The emergence and consolidation of Jewish community consciousness throughout the en-

tire period of the growth of Zionism brought with it a ten-
dency to overlook the presence of other people on the territory of the "homeland." Before 1903, Israel Zangwell is believed to have been the first to proclaim that Zion was "a land
without a people for a people without a land." This narcissistic disacknowledgment of the "other," driven by the extrem-
ity of need and by the intense investment of self in the Zionist
ideal and in the Israeli State, has, as we have seen, contributed to Palestinian Arab rage and many of the crises experienced by the new state of Israel. Our data demonstrate that
the tendency toward "de-recognition" of non-Jewish peoples
in Israel is gradually becoming modified among some
Israelis—still a distinct minority—by growth of appreciation
for Arab perspectives. This kind of attitudinal change can be
identified among some specialists on Arab outlook and politics. We will return to this issue.

In May, 1948, when Israel declared its independence, it
counted 759,000 instant citizens. By 1975, despite four wars,
its total population had grown by natural increase and by
ingathering and integration of Jews from many countries to
3,240,000 of whom 85 percent were Jewish. In the first 25
years, 1,517,900 immigrants arrived. In the first three years
after independence, 754,800 emigrated to Israel, mostly
from Europe and the Arab countries. A further 165,000
Jews came from Morocco, Tunisia, and Poland between 1955
and 1957. Another wave of 262,000 immigrants came mainly
from North and South America, Western Europe and the
Soviet Union between 1967 and 1973. All these people had
to learn the Hebrew language to be integrated into the society. New towns and cities had to be built. Agriculture had to
be revived, industry established. The defense needs of the
country had to be met and *were* met by the development of a
massive citizens' armed forces that could be mobilized
quickly in time of need.

Meanwhile, the Arab minority also had to be served. Its

population grew to 476,900 in 1973; the literacy rate among Arab citizens of Israel rose considerably in those same years; life expectancy increased from 52 to 72 years; the school population multiplied ten times; the number of Arab students attending the university rose from 15 to 1,200. Israel is proud of this record. Its spokesmen point to the improvement in the quality of life of Arab citizens, their access to the political system, their relative advantages in comparison with people in neighboring Arab states. Nonetheless, Arab citizens of Israel continue to complain of "second-class citizenship" and sometimes to press for the establishment of a Palestinian Arab entity. There have been many incidents of rioting by Arabs in Israel, as well as providing shelter for terrorists and information to Israel's enemies. Some Arabs have been imprisoned for treasonous crimes against the state and this has been loudly protested in the world press. Arab citizen integration is less than certain, less than complete.

Even more uncertain is the dilemma of the administered areas—territories occupied in the Six-Day War of 1967; the West Bank of Jordan, and Gaza Strip, Sinai, and the Golan Heights. About one million Arab people live in these areas, predominantly Moslems, with a minority of Christians. The basic policy of Israel has been to encourage cooperation between the Arabs of the occupied areas and Israelis and to maintain an "open bridges" arrangement allowing movement of people and goods between the administered areas and Arab countries. Nevertheless, there have been accusations of heavy-handedness whenever the Arab peoples have been less than cooperative; the standard response to sheltering of terrorists has been to destroy the buildings which provided shelter. Israeli officials argue that this is less final than killing people; Arab administered people find the policy ultimately ruthless, especially when Israeli settlement has been permitted in certain occupied areas.

Despite these major and very complex problems, the na-

tion of Israel has sustained a process of growth, development, and accomplishment quite unique in history. The new
Israelis generally present a pioneering aspect, with a willingness to work hard to make innovations work. Upgrading of
agriculture is a case in point. It started with the socialist
models of the Kibbutz and the private cooperative idea of the
Moshav. Both forms of village enterprise have explored the
most ancient forms of agricultural economy side by side with
contemporary and advanced technological innovation—a
luxury permitted to a people not bound by tradition but
respectful of the discoveries of the past. For example, ancient
forms of terracing have been supplemented by advanced
forms of delivery of scarce water and nutrients. Israel ex-
ports agricultural products, especially luxury fruits, at the
same time that nearly 85 percent of the population is ur-
banized. It provides goods and services to the population and
especially to tourists, who, along with overseas remittances,
provide a very substantial proportion of foreign exchange.

In addition to the development of the nation, Israel has
sent a considerable number of technical assistance missions
to other nations, including the Middle East (Iran), Sub-
Saharan Africa, Southeast Asia, and even Japan.

This relatively small nation, with limited resources, sur-
rounded by hostile nation-states, has managed to survive
through almost total self-involvement of the people with the
nation and the committed support of Jews in other countries.
External relations have been profoundly affected by the
commitment of Diaspora Jews to Israel's survival, especially
the eight million Jews of the United States. Israel is a modern
nation-state, however sparse her resources, tied firmly to the
Western democratic-socialist civilization in both spirit and
politics. Israel continues to have a "special affinity" to the
United States, despite recurrent strains in the relationship.

Israeli attachment—the co-mingling of self and nation

Of all the psychological elements in Israeli behavior, the deepest and most fundamental appears to be the patriotic attachment to the nation, an attachment so profound as to be virtually inseparable from the self of the Israeli citizen. We have observed this attachment in many circumstances, manifested in many ways, concealed behind the most sophisticated rationalizations. We have also been impressed with this same quality of psychological attachment to Israel among non-Zionist Jews in the United States who have commented to us that they seriously considered volunteering to fight for Israel during such crises as the 1973 War, although they were anything but soldiers.

For a great many Jews inside and outside Israel, the establishment of the State of Israel led almost immediately to a very personal and fundamental expansion of the extended self to the State. This condition we have termed a narcissistic hypercathexis of the State. This is not surprising in retrospect; a large number of persons who had suffered persecution and even self-hatred for their adherence to a faith and people were suddenly provided with a basis for pride. Collective and personal self-esteem rose simultaneously; a people with millenia of humiliation and relative helplessness were now free-standing among the other peoples of the world. We might illustrate these points by describing the case of Yuri.

The time was 1970. Yuri M., a personal friend of 14 years, consented to an interview for this project. Fifteen minutes into the interview, an entirely unexpected outburst occurred. The question had seemed innocuous enough, especially since the interviewer knew that Yuri had just returned from a technical mission to strengthen the Bar-Lev line guarding the Sinai and had complained about the necessity. "Look, Yuri, don't you think it's time for the political leadership to consider mediation on that border would be to Israel's ad-

vantage and perhaps Egypt's too? Both countries are suffering, you know."

Then the outburst. "Don't you know that I came to
Israel—then Palestine—at ten years of age after a year away
from my family in Germany. Don't you know that both of my
parents died, I don't know how, in the Holocaust. You don't
know what it is to be helpless, to give in, to depend on the
good-will of others, to be betrayed, to be mistaken, to lose
your family, to be left alone. No, No, No! I can never take
anything on trust—from anybody. No, I don't believe in
mediation, even over that worthless ground. What I believe
in is what I can defend, what depends on no one else and
certainly not on a promise. No, the political leadership
should not accept mediation, should not accept promises,
should not accept guarantees, even from America. We have
had enough of them. I had enough of them. Now you know
what it has cost me. Yes, I hate to go into the Sinai. Yes, I
think this border on Suez is insane. But don't ask me to trust.
I don't hate Arabs or Egypt, but I don't trust them either. So
I'll go to Sinai. I'll do whatever is necessary until I know that
Israel is safe, safe by its own strength, safe without the promises of others. When Egypt makes peace, when it disarms its
borders, when it permits our surveillance, then and not until
then should we make adjustments."

The outburst died down, his hands stopped trembling,
and Yuri gradually returned to the thoughtful, friendly,
judicious man that the interviewer had known so long. But a
raw nerve had been touched and we both knew it. Yuri's
name had been Maximillian in Germany, his family had been
assimilated; he knew he was a Jew but didn't think much
about that. In 1938 his family became worried. When they
sent him to relatives in Italy he thought it was for a visit. He
was sent on to Palestine in 1939 to stay with other more
distant relatives. Letters from home stopped coming in 1940
when he was eleven years old. He never saw his parents

again. Of a large extended family only an uncle had some-how survived. By the time he was fifteen years old he was quite certain that his parents had died. The news and rumors all said so; besides they would not have lost touch if there were any possible way. And it was clear that if they had died, it was because they were Jews. Yuri adopted his Hebrew name. He forgot nothing. He just protected a painful truth from the outside world, and he determined to live as a man, a Jew, an Israeli.

Big, gentle, talented, Yuri and his Sabra wife, Petra, re-turned to Israel where he has continued a distinguished career. They have two vigorous children. They and their two children live in Tel Aviv, their living conditions Spartan and difficult by American standards. Both work; neither is well paid by American standards and they are heavily taxed. Yuri is prominent in his field. He is a consummate technician, sought by foreign firms. He is sophisticated in every sense, versed in the arts, a rational and non-polemic conver-sationalist, scarcely imaginable as an impassioned patriot, a good friend numbering foreigners and non-Jews among his close acquaintances.

To know the other side of Yuri, the deep and determined commitment to Israel, the depth of self-involvement seldom shown, never displayed, was a rare privilege. Yuri works hard at his profession and his achievements add to the luster of his country. He raises his children as Israelis, independent and fearless. He provides his considerable skills to the de-fense of the State. As the outburst we have described indi-cates, his identification with Israel is very deep: a political inquiry triggered a forceful account of his own life experi-ences. The central issue is self-reliance, autonomy, and a resolution not to be again injured, humiliated, or let down by dependence on others. Ordinarily, he would not care about geographic boundaries, although he works in their defense. These are negotiable to him, but only under circumstances of direct, man-to-man, state-to-state contact and only under circumstances that do not endanger the security of Israel. From the standpoint of those who would press the Yuris of Israel for concessions, such persons are considered fundamentally rigid and intransigent. Those who know Yuri differently, who understand how the deeply felt meanings of self and state are intertwined in people like him, would find him both fair and reliable. The interviewer learned from others that Yuri had been a hero in the War of Independence, but he would not speak of it himself.

The transformation from Jew of the Diaspora to Israeli Jew entails not only individually variable cultural, social, and religious elements but also a transformation of self and narcissism which is highly maturational. In many instances it is a rebirth or reenergizing of the personality, and sometimes virtually a metamorphosis of "Saul to Paul" dimensions. In the aggregate of millions it may in part account for the accomplishments of Israeli industry. It is not possible for us to offer here any large number of individual life histories in support of this impression, but the following example is rather typical and is balanced by a somewhat different reaction on the part of the spouse.

Sophie was born and raised in the Diaspora as were generations of her family before her. Her father had come to Egypt from Turkey but she had known only Egypt throughout her youth. Her father, and her mother in conformity with him, lived a moderately religious life. As a child, Sophie attended a Hebrew school once a week, where she learned some Jewish history and Hebrew. She paid little attention to these studies. Her regular school was international and conducted in French; her schoolmates included many upper class Moslems. Her father had a managerial position in a large commercial concern which was owned and operated by Jews who were well accepted by the Egyptians, though not assimilated. The entire family lived in close contact with the international element of Cairo society. The father, well-off but not rich, provided amply for his family. Sophie grew up before World War II with the luxury of numerous servants, few responsibilities, and ample time to enjoy an active social life. Her family and the culture put much greater emphasis on her attractive physical appearance and her self-indulgence than on her innate high intelligence and creative capacity; these were largely unappreciated and undeveloped.

Growing up in these circumstances, it is not surprising that Sophie gave little thought to international affairs or the position of the large Jewish community in Egypt. There was a short-lived stirring of awareness of these issues in 1948 with the establishment of the state of Israel, but the Jews who emigrated to Israel at that time were mostly not so well-off and personally unknown to her. She continued in what she described as the "dream life." After her marriage to a young non-religious Jew with a promising career ahead of him, they joined a social and sports club with a broad range of membership: Egyptians, Jews, and many internationals, especially English and French. Among their friends were several Egyptian Army officers. Sophie had little consciousness of national or ethnic identity, but in retrospect she reports that she thought of herself as, "Egyptian . . . well, no, Jewish from Egypt." The dream life continued until 1956. If she thought at all about the history of the Jewish people it was that, "nothing will happen to us. It was like being asleep. No, even more, chloroformed like the Romans. Although we did not live in a ghetto, we felt that in a way we had our country within a bigger country."

The war of 1956 began for her with some fear about the bombing, but this was overshadowed within a day or two by her husband's arrest. Suspected of secretly helping the Zionists, he was placed in a concentration camp. All of this came just at the time she was quite excited about moving to a new and large apartment. Her husband had done well as an employee of a large commercial operation, but unlike her father's this one was Egyptian controlled. Very shortly after her husband's arrest and internment, a policeman came to inform her that she must leave the country with her three young children within 48 hours. She was already frantic at her husband's arrest and apparent disappearance and the loss of her apartment, her automobile, money in the bank, jewelry, etc., which she would not be permitted to take with her. Now she felt she was going crazy. In the street she met others, English, French, as well as Jews who were under the same 48-hour ultimatum. A meeting was held by the Red Cross for the victims of this ultimatum, and through this effort a two-month extension of the deportation order was granted. Appeals to Egyptian friends for help in locating her husband were turned aside with agonized pleas not to endanger them with the authorities by making further calls.

From official sources she found out where her husband was interned and was permitted to bring him clean clothes and medical supplies and pick up laundry each week. But she was not allowed to see him. In the meantime, she tried to dispose of her property, to buy clothing, and to select some few items of jewelry which she would be permitted to take from the country. She felt depressed because her prized goods had suddenly lost their value; a refrigerator was worth no more than five dollars. Worse still, she remembers Moslems coming to the house and saying, "I want this and this." In time she learned to cope by saying, "it's sold." Later the French and English who were expelled received financial compensation for their property. Sophie felt deeply the loss of her money and cherished things. In the long run she was to find Israel a satisfying compensation.

One day an Egyptian soldier came to their home. They were afraid he had come to kill them, but instead he brought a letter from her husband. He did so for money—which he got at both ends. She learned from her husband that he was getting bad food, cold water showers in the middle of winter, and no medical supplies. But he had not been subjected to brutality.

When she arrived with their children at the boat assigned to them by the Red Cross she found her husband; he was thin, cold, grey, and very tense. They were bound for Naples from which the refugees would transship to Israel or any of the large number of nations which had offered to receive them. Her husband was attracted to Brazil but Sophie was already leaning to Israel. "On the boat something happened. When we got outside Egyptian waters, people began to sing Jewish songs." She told her husband, "if you go to Brazil, you go alone. I am going with the children to Israel." He readily agreed. In Naples they were met by representatives of many Kibbutzim. Sophie and the family went for a short period to a kibbutz where her brother was located. Her husband went to study Hebrew. The little Hebrew she had learned as a child and a natural talent for languages enabled her quickly to learn the language. After three months they were assigned a small house in the country which was furnished with orange crate simplicity. She keeps one grey blanket as a souvenir of those days.

Heroic efforts to adjust without complaint to the Spartan country life were not successful and she developed numerous physical complaints. Finally the doctor told her that she must go to the city where, "I would be better understood."

They settled in Tel Aviv where they were happier, though they still had adjustment problems to face. The basic adjustment, however, was accomplished rapidly and constituted a transformation in her entire way of life, attitude and values; "In Israel another woman was born." She washed, cooked, sewed, and did everything for herself and the family, things she had never before had to do. She found life intensely ascetic but this was alleviated by a growing feeling of national identity. A constant stimulus to this transformation was the memory of the Egyptian policeman coming to her home to inform her she had to leave the country within 48 hours. She marvelled at her former naivete and her astonishment, "How can he say this? He can't mean it, my house, my country." Her feeling of Jewishness was enormously enhanced in Israel by her association with other Jews. She laughingly commented that they had felt very keenly that in Israel there were too many Jews. "You have only Jews to deal with, and they all are smart; it's much harder."

One of the things that makes Sophie feel at home in Israel is her friendship with women who have had similar experiences. In place of the former superficial relations she now felt kinship. In her flight to Israel she lost her belongings but discovered belonging. The change of cathexis from clothes, jewelry, and household furnishings to people, culture, and nation resulted in a broadening of her personality and in turn the development of a different life which has brought her much happiness. She sees gratitude as one of the wellsprings of her patriotism. She also feels she must never again be a foreigner. Sharing vicariously in her children's development as Israelis has helped consolidate her new identification. Her son's active duty in the two latest wars was a final confirmation.

"Israel became a part of me, its culture, especially the music, and even to some extent the religion." When she and her husband were assigned to overseas missions she would often play Israeli music in the morning and would weep tears of joy and nostalgia.

Even though Sophie's husband by nature was very adaptable and accustomed from his job in Egypt to dealing with non-Jews, he found Israel a "tremendous shock." He constantly felt he was up against the entrenched Ashkenazim establishment. Relegated to a lesser job by the relocation, he slowly began to feel more at home however and achieved steady promotion. Although they were considered and con-

sidered themselves Oriental Jews, they never felt the necessity to emulate the many immigrants from Iraq who "constructed their Baghdad Ghetto in Israel as the German Jews
did in Naharia and the Romanians did in Ramli and parts of
Beersheba."

Sophie's husband is devoted to Israel but remains basically
a cosmopolitan and still thinks it possible that he may settle in
some other part of the world. For Sophie there is only one
realistic possibility. She thinks of her husband as still being a
bit of a dreamer, but she knows that there is only one home
for her: Israel. She has only to remember the policeman at
the door to renew her conviction that Israel must continue to
be her home, her country.

Group reinforcement of attachment to the land and the
state of Israel especially characterizes the pioneers; those
who came to Palestine to build the basis for a Jewish homeland.

In 1960, one of us was the guest at a dinner given by an
Israeli club. Fourteen members enjoyed an elegant meal in
old-world surroundings carefully constructed in a working
industrial building. The dinner was the prelude to a long
and far-ranging discussion about the past and future of
Israel. The members, who met every two weeks, were all past
middle life and all held positions of responsibility in Israeli
society as leaders of the country's industrial, commercial, and
intellectual institutions. Their personal histories were re-
markably similar in broad outline; they had come to Palestine
from Germany in the late 1920's and early 30's because of
their socialist ideals and Zionist commitment. They had all
come from solidly established European families and had
university educations. There was a powerful romanticism in
their emigration which was still evident among them after
more than thirty years of utterly realistic and often harsh and
dangerous existence.

When these men came to Palestine, they had sought and

found places for useful manual labor as was required by the socialist work ethic. They drove buses, drained swamps, and tilled the soil. Some of the technically trained built the simplest sort of labor-extending devices such as pumping and tillage systems. Each of these men had spent at least five years in such activity before they yielded to the obvious need for their skills and talents at higher organizational levels. They were unanimous in their regret at the passing of their pioneer days.

Every member of this group had participated in the War of Independence in positions of substantial military, industrial, or governmental leadership. For years they had organized the military capacity of the Haganah, the underground army, and provided sinews of logistical and financial support for it. This no longer interested them much . It was taken for granted and tales of war-companionship were much less nostalgic than those of the pioneering days. They did, however, offer a silent toast to companions who had died in the wars.

We will comment on only two of the items of this long discourse, which, in fact, continues to the present day. The members were concerned with their observations of developing trends in Israeli society, and they were greatly stimulated by their guest's acquaintance with Arab and Palestinian developments. Perhaps the most remarkable aspect of this occasion was the degree to which men who had been meeting so long were thinking freshly and were attentive to each other's views. There was nothing stale, nothing canned or repetitious about various positions; one of the reinforcing norms of the group was to explore new ideas, to think forwardly.

Perhaps the key to consideration of the development of Israeli society may be found in the gift of a privately printed edition of Theodor Herzl's *Altneuland* that the visitor was presented with at the end of the evening. For it became clear

that the constant concern of these men was the integration
and synthesis of past and future history. The depth of investment of the lives and selves of these founders of Israel
became evident; they were secular men but their devotion to
their country was distinctly religious in character. As one of
them said, "We have given our lives to Israel, that is true, but
it is not all that heroic when you consider that Israel has
given our lives to us—and they are good lives."

Our conversation foreshadowed many of the issues which
were later described in Amos Elon's work on *The Israelis:
Founders and Sons*[1] and many other writings. It was clear to
these men that the pioneering days were passing and that the
newer generation was more self-concerned and possibly less
committed to the State, at least in the old utopian sense. How
would consumerism, corruption, welfarism, and personal
self-seeking affect the future? Would Israelis want to stay in
Israel and face the deprivations of permanent nation-
building? Would the increasing levels of educational availability detach young Israelis from simple commitment? How
could the State meet the problems of structural injustice in
distribution of privilege—especially with respect to Oriental
immigrants?

We will not outline the answers as none were really found.
But it is notable that there was very little use of derivative
theory or political philosophy despite obvious acquaintance
with these ideas and world experience in implementing
them. The bedrock ideals of socialism and Zionism did not
require discussion. They were assumed. But beyond that the
members were concerned with helping to create a distinctly
new and genuinely Israeli society. The problem was how to
blend intense pragmatism with idealism and the question was
always: what ideas could provide guiding principles worthy
of universal adherence? They did not find answers that evening but they were able to discard religious and classic
capitalist—and less certainly, communal—socio-economic

models among others. We were left with ideals of continuous seeking of social justice, at least within the nation, and a realization that commitment to the State itself was the most fundamental motivation for social cohesion. They held this commitment themselves, but it was difficult to imagine how it would be sustained in coming generations. They believed it could be.

With respect to relations with Palestinians and other Arabs, there was an extended discussion of the need for the limits of contact and cooperation. Each of these men had had extensive personal contact with Palestinian Arabs, often in working places and in functional friendships. They had found limits in these friendships and did not suppose that any political structure or purpose could genuinely integrate Jew and Arab; a considerable number of personal experiences had shown that the most basic loyalties were to one's own people. In fact, the consensus was of regretful respect for this "truth."

The discussion became intense and the questioning of the visitor was searching, detailed, and attentive. Both internal and external Arab sentiments and actions were of profound interest. Reports of police state aspects of Egyptian society were exceedingly distressing (this was 1960), a clear identification of Nasser with Hitler became evident and the previous clarity of discussion was somewhat disrupted. As the subject of Nasser's alleged utilization of former Nazi propagandists was broached by one of the members, there was a full and complete flowering of all the phenomena of what has been called group paranoia, especially an absolute certainty that the main focus of Nasser and the Egyptian society was, indeed had to be, the destruction of Israel and all her people. Accompanying this there was a steely determination to sustain such strength as to insure that there would be no possibility of successful attacks on Israel, military or political. In the latter context, the role of the UN in its peace-keeping functions was severely castigated; neither the UN nor any level of world opinion or pressure would sway Israel; it was regretted that Israel had withdrawn from Sinai after the 1956 War; "What did that get us but more exposure to danger?"*

Quite naturally, as this evening's multilogue unfolded, there arose a consensus that Israel could and would defend herself. Now, we all recognized that much of the earlier conversation about future development of Israeli society had been stimulated by the central concern of the survival of Israel in a hostile environment. Much of the speculation and worry had been about whether, in an evolving society, there would be the commitment and the strength that these founders had needed. It was a relief to the group to rediscover this connection and to affirm their confidence that the rising generation, no matter how different its attitudes might be, would share the commitment with certainty. After all, the selves of young Israelis (we did not use the term self at this time but its meaning was clearly implied) were, if anything, even more fundamentally integrated with the nation.

Instead of multiplying examples of the intimate connection of personal selves with the nation of Israel—there are literally dozens of individually fascinating life stories in this respect—we will only comment here that the mechanism of merger with the omnipotent object, that is, with the nation as a self-object, resulted in a heroic idealizing of nation which was manifested in action, thus permitting a personal modesty

* Parenthetically, and to anticipate later developments, one of this committee was able to review group dynamic considerations in Jerusalem a decade later and to discuss this evening's conversation with some of the participants in it. Nasser's defeat in 1967 had made a great difference; it was not recognized that he had been the object of stereotyping by displacement of the image from Adolph Hitler. There was some reconsideration of whether Nasser might not, after all, be "moderate" on the question of Israel's survival. Since that time and especially after Nasser's death, there has been a thorough reassessment of Nasser's political and military intentions toward Israel and even rueful regret that some response had not been attempted.

coupled with profound enhancement of satisfaction in one's membership in the nation, especially of its status as a recognized State. Instant international recognition of Israel on its founding is still a source of deep pleasure to this generation of Israelis and to almost all Jews throughout the world. What accompanied this, as shown in the material, is a basic commitment to the survival of the state, conceived of as inseparably linked with survival of the self. The comments of our subjects also suggest that the memory of previous humiliation of Jews contributed to a degree of rage (although this was better balanced by pride in accomplishment than was the situation which we have described for the Palestine Arabs) which, coupled with continuing threat, both real and exaggerated, contributed to focusing on the enemy. Most specifically, this was focused on the person of Gamal Abdel Nasser. This very intimate emotion almost certainly contributed significantly to the policy decision to undertake the preemptive Sinai War of 1956 which perpetuated the cycle of conflict between Israel and her neighbors.

Let us now consider how some of the "sons," the generation of new immigrants and children of the founders have integrated the nation into their extended selves. The later immigrants' experience differed from that of the early pioneers, who had the common goal of creating a new culture. Separated usually from his parents, the pioneer did not experience conflict and rebellion between generations. His emigration to Israel often enabled him to realize intense youthful aspirations; asceticism and personal sacrifice were necessary for success. He was able to set up a socialist community, and this new community's cultural creativity—especially in its rejuvenation of the Hebrew language—bridged the historic, geographic, and ideologic distance from his parents, giving him both independence and a sense of continuity.[2] His religion provided support in the identification of Jews as a special definable group and through its tradition of community rather than individual salvation. Finally, the needs of the state and the pioneer were compatible. The pioneer was vital to the state's survival, while the state filled the pioneer's need for a country of his own.

Some of these factors still exist for the new immigrant entering the structured society of Israel. He is still vital to the state's survival and the state still represents a haven for him. This compatibility of needs is informally assisted by the special warmth of interaction between the immigrant and the absorbing society. Impersonal bureaucratization is impossible in such a relationship. But increasingly, disparity has developed between the pioneering ideology and social reality. The pioneering ideology emphasized equality, simplicity, and manual labor, but the new state has developed into a consumer society. Occupations and living standards have become differentiated, and inequalities have appeared. For instance, agricultural work, which was crucial in the pioneering ideology, has moved much lower on the list of occupational choices. Agricultural work and unskilled public services are often provided by Asian and North African immigrants, while western immigrants occupy the upper and middle echelons of public service. This is a generalization, of course, as length of residence rather than country of origin determines the distribution of workers in some fields.[3] Even with these problems, Israel suffers less from social inequalities than most other nations, which may be attributed to its source in socialist ideology.

Oriental immigrant groups tend to experience more serious problems of income instability and status insecurity than immigrants from Europe. Unlike western groups they have not been as readily integrated into Israeli society, and the characteristic symptoms of unassimilated status have emerged: increased juvenile delinquency, comparatively high crime rate, and family instability. What produced this lack of integration and its attendant problems? First, this group's educational and occupational achievements were less than the standards of the society that received it. Second, the Oriental immigrant family experienced a profound erosion of values. The father's role as unquestioned head of the family was often undermined. The sons grasped social realities such as *sochnut* (Jewish agency) and *Histadrut* (labor union) far more easily than the father; youths adapted more easily to the changed life style of Israeli society than bewildered parents struggling with the mysteries of a new environment. In addition, Israel needed the young more than the old. Because the older age group was assimilated with greater difficulty and was seen as less necessary to the society than the young, the authority of family elders deteriorated, sometimes precipitously.[4]

Soviet immigrants, who are welcomed and integrated into Israeli society through massive efforts by the Israeli government, elicit quite different responses among Israelis. Young men and women who have completed their military service find it practically impossible to obtain an apartment because so many apartments have been set aside for the new immigrants from the Soviet Union. They know that their government's commitment to Soviet immigration is part of the same determination which made possible the foundation of their State, but this knowledge clashes—like many other things in today's Israel—with the demands of a consumer society, with human nature, and with social justice.[5]

Israel has a population dilemma. Forty-four percent of its children are produced by 13 percent of its population, and Oriental Jewish families have a comparatively high birthrate. Birth control is problematical for Israel, which depends for survival on population increase and still mourns the two million children lost in the World War II Holocaust.

As Israeli society moves away from its pioneering origin, new problems appear. The present Zionist movement, for instance, is unable to reinterpret Zionism for present-day

Israel. Religion has become a complex issue. Only a minority of the population fully accepts the rabbinate as a source of authority, yet the rabbinate has general legal control over the entire Jewish population of Israel. It even determines which citizens are Jews.

Despite these difficulties and strains within Israeli society, and despite the fact that new immigrants do not entirely share the deep involvement, the total commitment of the pioneers, there is virtually universal shared self-involvement with the nation. The fate of all the inhabitants is a common one, as all are exposed to the same external threats and internal acts of terrorism. All Israelis, old and new, recognize the mutuality of their existence with that of the State; they depend on it and it depends on them. Much of the time, this self-involvement is silent and unspoken, but whenever a crisis arises it becomes highly visible. The entire population becomes vigilant and alert with each new terrorist incursion or each threat of war. The entire population becomes glued to the radio at such times of crisis; in public places the hourly news is attended to in dead silence and often expressions of agony or of triumph are freely displayed in response to turns of fortune. Never was this truer than during the October War of 1973, as the news provoked intense and spontaneous expressions of feeling, from deep anxiety to gradual triumph, to mourning the dead and celebrating the living.

A somewhat different sense of commitment is evident among the youth of Israel, those who have grown to adulthood within the State. Young Israelis—we interviewed many of them in universities and a special sample in the United States as reported in the Appendix—have grown up as Israelis, speaking Hebrew as their mother language, the first generation to do so. With the language, they absorbed the history of their people and most especially the short but eventful history of their country. Their sense of Israeli pride is deeply imbedded.

The preoccupations of the young Israeli adults are strikingly different from their forebears. They seem to be more
concerned with the here and now; the problems of housing,
of living, of careers. It is only on probing and questioning
that interviewers—at least non-Israelis—discover something
that appears to be taken for granted, that the rising generation is so deeply involved with their country as not to either
question or feel any need to explain it.

When our committee reviewed its interviews with young
Israelis, we were struck by the absence of biographical material, since as psychiatrists this kind of information had been
our prime and natural interest. This was all the more striking
as there was considerable openness to describing their
families and their backgrounds and as nearly all of them,
including many young women, had undergone military
training. A number of them served in the October War, but
any reference to it was laconic, and accepted as a fact of life.
In fact, we have found it uninstructive to describe biographical material in the personal sense; not that it is uninteresting,
but that almost all young people whom we interviewed in
sharp contrast to their parents took their nationality and its
demands so much for granted as to be considered irrelevant
to their personal histories and lives. Therefore, both here
and in the Appendix, we will only describe some of the
common experiences and attitudes.

The preoccupations of Israeli youth from as early as 1960
onward were almost entirely with the struggles of life: the
development of their studies and careers, the problems of
obtaining housing (especially when a young couple considered marriage), and the very real economic struggles that
they almost all experienced. They were aware of the limits of
parental support and determined not to be dependent. At
the next level of interest, young Israelis—at least those in
university life—were actively concerned about conditions of
life for themselves. They were sharply critical of administra-

tive arrangements, scholarship systems, housing and eating arrangements, and questions of justice within the educational system. They would organize protest groups to press for reforms. At this level, they seemed to turn more to the government and to institutional administrations than to their parents. Shortcomings were seen less as personal problems than as administrative failures that ought to be corrected. After 1968, they became increasingly critical of the habits of "protectzia"—small bribery for privilege—that they felt was an all too common practice. Political debate concerning these matters was active and partisan; it was also more practical than theoretical and was concerned with what should be done to remedy defects rather than principles of governance or social organization. In no place have we heard more convincing quotations of statistics in support of a position.

There were other types of young people whom we did not interview in depth, but merely observed and had passing contact with. These included Oriental Jews, whose number was not great at universities, but who tended to assume the responsibilities of adult life at an early age and at relatively simple occupational levels.

Underlying these surface concerns of daily life, however, was a depth of knowledge and assumed commitment to the nation that was all the more impressive for being undemonstrative. While such feelings appeared close to the surface in the pioneers, it was usually elicited only by direct questioning. In fact, it proved less difficult to elicit this material in group interviews than in individual discussion. One hears a good deal of complaint about the difficulties of life in Israel. But the first and most consistent response, when asked if emigration is being considered, typically would be: "Of course not. Israel is my country. Sure, we have a lot of troubles and we've made mistakes. But, good or bad, we know where we belong, who we are. We're Israelis and that's all there is to it. Besides, if life is hard here, we're very free

people. Life has trouble everywhere, especially for Jews.
We'll solve our problems—not perfectly, of course, but bit by
bit." Assertions like this were frequently followed by comments on the problems of other countries: lack of freedom in
Russia, the turmoil and dangers of the United States, political decay in West European countries. The Arab countries
were hardly worth comment, at least before 1973.

Israeli youth demonstrated a degree of awareness of
world-wide conditions and an alertness to political and social
developments quite unusual among university students. This
line of discussion often led to a review of the internal development of Israeli society and economy, and again the depth
of knowledge was impressive. Most of our subjects had visited many areas of the country and had observed the range
of agricultural and industrial activity firsthand. Finally, our
subjects would add a contingency concerning the future development of the nation: the threat of another war.

Most of the young people we interviewed had undergone
military training. They had gone on maneuvers in many
parts of the country and had discussed strategies, tactics, and
the political climate. They were quite expert in the weapons
capabilities of Israel—which they didn't talk about in any
detail—and of neighboring countries—which they did
discuss—especially anti-aircraft defense after 1973. There
was unanimity that each of them would do what they were
called upon to do in any military crisis. But until the moment
of need, questioning and debate about the wisdom of the
government and leadership were intense and anything but
unanimous. The younger generation felt on the whole that
they had inherited the consequences of leadership rigidity in
its international dealings, especially with respect to the Palestine Arabs. After the terrorist attacks beginning in 1968, we
heard a number of comments to the effect that Israel's
policies had forced this situation on the Arabs; that more
enlightened policies could have reduced the risks. These

youths were by no means dovish or pacifist, but regarded themselves as realists and their parents as unduly anxious and therefore rigid. These attitudes were strikingly at variance with both official stances and the reasoning of the older generation.

After the 1973 War, too, youth tended to be exceedingly critical of the leadership, of intelligence failures, of failure of alertness. They, after all, had paid a large part of the price of 2,500 dead as well as chagrin in battle, especially of the previously much-vaunted air force. Here, the great majority were absolutely unsparing of their elders and ruthlessly realistic in their calculations for the future. They recognized a gradually shifting balance of force in their region but did not entirely share their leaders' catastrophic outlook. They tended to be more confident of Israel's capacity to survive and less sensitively reactive to Arab rhetoric, especially the oft-quoted statements of previous decades that the Arab purpose was the total elimination of Israel. After 1973, there emerged a certain tendency among some Israelis—though still a small minority—to consider that peace and security for Israel, certainly the most desired goal, could not be ensured by strength of arms alone, but that more flexible postures toward indirect and direct contact and negotiations should be pursued. This was in some instances extended to include Palestinians. Significant numbers of Israeli youth have learned at least some Arabic and have developed some social contact with Arabs in Israel. They are less prone to accept polarized adversary images.

In reviewing this material, we were struck by the degree to which the representation of the nation itself had become internalized in the self-system of the native-born first generation Israelis. The nation was treated not only as a real external object but also as a coherent extension of the person, a central aspect of self. In fact, confidence in the nation and in themselves as nationals often appeared to be a relatively enduring component of the individual's self-esteem. Some young Israelis who were shy, troubled, or conflicted in their personal relations, and who appeared to suffer from personal self-doubt and sensitivity, would nevertheless demonstrate striking certainty about themselves as Israelis. In fact, it is probably true that the development of personal self-esteem and confidence has been greatly enhanced for a great many of this generation by the sense of pride and accomplishment associated with being an important part of the nation, just as the nation is an important part of them. In this dynamic of development, young Israelis are almost the opposite of their parents. While the parents solved massive problems of personal survival and overcame fears of humiliation or weakness by national commitment, the new generation has incorporated elements of strength, confidence, and pride from their self-involvement. Simultaneously and inevitably, they also have internalized the problems of national survival and welfare. The internalization of national identity as a central element of the self, consolidated over and over again by the experience of wars and crises, appears to provide both an anchoring point from which internal and external events are measured and a stimulus to development and action consonant with that identity. Although there are individual exceptions, the sense of national selfhood is a source of confidence and purpose for the majority of Israeli youth.

National crisis and the response of self

The overwhelming intellectual and emotional involvement of Israelis with their country that we have described provides the constant backdrop against which international events are experienced and responded to. While there is constant dissection of the acts of government, and criticism and self-criticism of internal development in times of relative peace, the shared self-involvement with the nation becomes evident in times of threat or crisis. As we have noted, the War of Independence had been fought both for the establishment and the survival of the nation. The Sinai War of 1956 was deliberate and concerted, a policy war intended to increase the security of the state and expressing also elements of rage at past and threatened humiliation. But the June War of 1967 and the October War of 1973 were of a different character. They were perceived by Israelis as external threats to the survival of the country and participation in those wars served as a consolidation of self-involvement with the nation state.

Once the external threat was apparent, the rapidity of mobilization of the whole nation, from fighting units to support and home-front activities, has been a much-noted phenomenon. While a good part of this capacity for rapid mobilization and instant shift to a war footing may be attributed to planning and training designed for total defense of a small and vulnerable country, the basic strength of emergency response depended on each individual unhesitatingly and whole-heartedly assuming the responsibilities of his or her role. Furthermore, the Israeli command system allows greater initiative and flexibility to each fighting unit than any other military force in modern history. Once tactical objectives are set, field units have unusual autonomy in adapting their actions to the changing requirements of their particular sectors. Moreover, each unit takes responsibility for its members. There are very few incidents of men deserting their group or of units abandoning their members.

Two conditions are required for these Israeli fighting methods: first, that every individual is fundamentally and personally involved in the nation and its objectives; and second, that each individual has a clear concept of the significance of his or her particular role. In times of crisis there is very little confusion in such matters; here, the functions of open communication throughout the nation become evident. Men at the fighting front and workers behind the lines are equally avid in following each development reported on the radio and have little difficulty relating their instructions through channels of military communication to the progress of the battle for national survival. Such response obviously goes far beyond the loyalty of subjects to military commands or of subordinates to authority; it represents total self-involvement with the nation.

The Wars of 1967 and 1973 were each followed by extensive reassessment and revision of the common national self-perception. The lightning victory of 1967 initiated a period of shared unrealistic overconfidence—even grandiosity—during which there was a widespread feeling of well-being and of cohesiveness within the nation. For the first time there was a sense of relative invulnerability, of firm existence in space—more defensible boundaries—and of durability. In terms of extended self-development, this brief era represents a progressive phase. The desperate fear of internal fragmentation or external penetration was relieved and a consolidated sense of integrity was established. There was substantial merger of individual selves with an idealized national image, sometimes accompanied by degrees of overestimation concerning national capacities.

The 1973 War administered an extremely sobering corrective. Although Israeli arms prevailed, it was at the price of rediscovery of the limits of superiority of men and units and of the degree of vulnerability of the nation. It is not accidental that the three elements of Israeli society that had been most heroically idealized—the military-political leadership, the air force, and the intelligence system—should be the most victimized by the events of October 1973 and the most severely criticized by popular reaction. In the following fifteen months during which our observations continued, a double process manifested itself. On the one hand, many

Israelis, especially the younger generation, still further consolidated their identity with the nation and some showed a
new maturity of self-confidence that permitted more realistic
recognition and even grudging admiration for non-Israeli
combatants. On the other hand, substantial numbers of Israelis went through periods of profound depression and
disillusionment and tended to regress toward extreme forms
of mystical nationalism containing at times elements of
fatalism about the ultimate triumph or destruction of the
state. Mistrust of Arabs and determination to maintain Israeli military superiority remained the dominant theme
among the majority of Israelis. What balance will be found
between these alternative solutions to the threat of fragmentation of the extended self under external pressure is still far
from evident. What is certain, however, is that the investment of self in the nation has been established to a degree
that the individual Israeli's extended self continues to be the
central focus for the organization of his or her activities.

The Six-Day war and the idealized state

The events preceding the Six-Day War of 1967 brought a
rapidly escalating sense of threat as forces gathered against
Israel's borders on several fronts. The closing of the Straits
of Tiran by Egypt in the face of international guarantees of
free passage for ships of all countries presented a direct
threat to Israel's survival and a clear *cassus belli*. When Israel
struck, first virtually destroying enemy air forces on the
ground and then enveloping both the Sinai and the Golan
Heights as well as the West Bank of the Jordan, the principal
border threats were eliminated by a dramatic military victory. Scarcely anyone in Israel had anticipated such a rapid
and thorough victory at so low a cost.

The collective sigh of relief at the successful conclusion of
the Six-Day War was followed almost immediately by an

almost unbelieving burst of pride. Returning soldiers, especially airmen, were greeted with special community celebration. For some time there was almost a reversal of generational authority; little credit was given to the government with the exception of the military leadership—especially Moshe Dayan—but there was extreme idealization of youthful combatants. The world press provided a very favorable mirror for Israeli accomplishments. An entirely new sort of grandiose, narcissistic humor appeared. For example, an Egyptian commander warns his battalion, "Be careful, there are two of them."

As the reality of Israel's victory was absorbed and integrated into the consciousness of her people, many experienced a new confidence in the nation and in themselves. There was a grandiose sense that "we can do anything." Earlier anxious and even desperate involvement with the nation became transformed into admiring idealization and a pride in citizenship. Along with this there appeared a capacity to work with enthusiasm and pleasure and with great effectiveness, an expansiveness that was manifested in projects for internal development in industry and agriculture and in greatly expanded international activities. Two attitudes that were somewhat new to Israeli outlooks also evolved quite rapidly: the first, a sense of autonomy and independence, a feeling of being able to "go it alone" with much less need for external support; the second, a new and almost sympathetic interest in Arab and even Palestinian affairs manifested by a great increase in the study of the language, culture, and politics of the Arab world. The latter was, of course, the outcome of the new self confidence which permitted a feeling of safety in dealing with adversaries and even a certain generosity toward them. Members of this committee who had previous acquaintance with Israelis were struck by the sudden lessening of defensiveness and of stereotyping and by the new level of seriousness with which a reassessment of Israeli-Arab relations was considered and discussed. There were new efforts to work out Israel's place in the Middle East and this was reflected in policies toward the million Arabs in the occupied territories and in cautious encouragement of increased trade and visits across the Jordanian boundary. Israelis began to want Arabs to see for themselves the progress of Israeli society. After the war, captured enemy soldiers were given tours before they were returned in prisoner exchanges.

This national self-confidence was manifested in the manner in which sabotage, bombings, and terrorist attacks were dealt with. A few months after the War, numerous bomb explosions occurred—in supermarkets, student dining halls, bus stations, cinemas. This was followed by the Arab "hijack war" of 1968. While prior to the June War such episodes had caused tremors of agitation throughout the country and had deterred some development undertakings, such episodes were now met with an attitude of resigned acceptance. Security forces were strengthened and their functions were trusted. A series of policies to contain terrorism was instituted even as the policy of retaliation across borders was abandoned. Programs of construction, especially in the cultural sphere—theaters, boutiques, beach resorts, hotels, universities—multiplied along with more fundamental work in urban development and redevelopment. Immigrants from western countries came in unprecedented numbers. In short, the dangers of terrorism and risk of war no longer threatened the integrity of the nation. They could be lived with and coped with in relative equanimity.

Representative of the "ordinary" middle class citizens whom we interviewed was a 37-year-old Sabra wife of an immigrant engineer from Middle Europe, the mother of three children, the oldest of whom had just begun military training. Mrs. L has never traveled outside Israel; she felt no need to do so and has never thought of living anywhere else.

She doesn't consider herself or her husband religious persons but simply Israelis. She is sharply critical of those orthodox Jewish communities who "don't contribute anything to the country and sometimes just make a lot of trouble." Nevertheless, her family participates in Holy Day observances.

In her personal life, Mrs. L considers herself essentially a housewife, although she works as a volunteer managing a summer camp for children and does part-time teaching. She also helped organize a day-care center out of dedication to Israeli children. Mrs. L has always been an active and energetic contributor to the welfare and development of her own community, quite consciously engaged in the development of the nation. "What we must have," she says, "is peace and development. Never before have we had real peace. Now for the first time (since 1967) we can feel safer; we don't have to spend all of our energies defending our borders. The army can take care of that. I'm proud that my son is in the army although we miss him at home. He comes home often and he is strong and confident, a real Israeli soldier." This attitude was prevalent during the post-1967 period. Many Israelis felt an extremely close link between building their own lives and the development and defense of their country.

With respect to relations to the Arab people and states, Mrs. L applied an Israeli solution: "Why can't the Arabs do the same for their own people as we do for ours? I can't imagine myself feeling at home as a minority group; I can't see why they even want to stay. After all, there is plenty of room for development in their countries. We feel strongly that we must take care of our new immigrants because they had no safety in the lands they came from. The same is true for the Arabs. The important thing is the lives of people, their health, development, education, welfare. The problem is with the Arab governments; why don't they create social reforms for their people instead of trying to destroy ours? If we develop ourselves and are strong, they will have to follow our example. Then there won't be much of a problem and relations will normalize. You know, I speak some Arabic and played with Arab children when I grew up and still have Arab acquaintances; they just want a decent life. Actually they are happy to be in Israel. At least it's good for them here." Mrs. L's optimism and confidence were, she admitted, greatly enhanced by the outcome of the 1967 War; before that she had "worried a lot more than I do now."

Another Israeli was considerably more thoughtful; a university official in his early fifties who had emigrated from Germany as a young man. The interviewer had known him since 1959. He was always a man of great self-confidence, an acknowledged leader and promoter of his university's national and world status, a man with a wide network of international intellectual connections. Prior to 1967, whenever he had met the interviewer, he had engaged him in a survey of global opportunities to find alliances and connections in the intellectual world that might contribute to a better understanding of Israel, to working relations that might strengthen support in the international scholarly and technical community. Always in these meetings, he also reviewed the position of Israel, its vulnerabilities in a military and political sense. Skillful and sophisticated as he was, he could not accept or sympathize with the support which he thought the UN and the world community, including the United States, gave to displaced Palestinian Arabs. He attributed a great deal of their activity to the "mistake" of sanctioning refugee status. His dream, which he frequently and wistfully described, was that somehow the Israeli experience with development of a neglected land could be transferred to former Palestinian Arabs in their host territories; that they, too, could make their deserts bloom and become truly resettled and have no wish to return. Indeed, his knowledge of possibilities for economic development of the Arab territories, where he had

never been, was impressive and convincing; the interviewer
thought it likely that Palestinian Arabs could create new lives
in their new places just as the new people of Israel had
done—if they wanted to. An extreme variant of this formula
was the idea that it might somehow be possible to bring
groups of Palestinians to Israel for technical training in agricultural and industrial development at a suitable level of
complexity; he was quite critical of the ill effects of education
in the most modern Western technologies.

The bottom line of this entire argument was, of course, to
move toward a circumstance in which the existence and security of Israel would be obtained by improvement in the life
circumstances of the former inhabitants of Palestine. As he
said, "As it is, they have nothing to lose." The official was too
diplomatic to say so bluntly, but it required very little ex-
trapolation to realize that he was convinced that the Western
democracies were failing, almost deliberately, to try to resolve the problems of the Middle East and particularly those
of the Palestinians; that those democracies were once again
manifesting a moral blindness toward the Jewish people and
toward their country.

In 1970 and 1972, when the interviewer again met with
this official, he had thoroughly reorganized his attitudes and
his activities. He was as urbane as ever, but much more
positive, gently letting the interviewer know who was the
host, no longer deferential. He no longer sought international support in the West but spoke of cooperation as a full
co-equal; a good deal of technical exchange was still under
his eye. He spoke of how much the United States in particular could learn from Israel, especially in the field of intermediate technology. If the United States were really to contribute to the less-developed nations, he made clear, it would
need to learn a lot; Israel and his institution would be pleased
to be the teacher. But his real focus now was neither on the
older democracies nor on Arab neighbors. He was scarcely

concerned with the Palestine Arabs despite their rising level
of activity against Israel. Rather, he had begun to conceive of
a new role and new alignment; one between Israel and
third-world countries. His reasoning was straightforward;
since 1967, neighboring Arab states were not an immediate
threat nor was it possible to negotiate with them. Israel could
adequately defend herself in the Middle East—she was beginning to make her own arms and was much less dependent
on the West. In fact, she was still rehabilitating captured
Russian equipment. The Palestinians were certainly a sore
point. They continued to annoy and to agitate, but there was
little trouble controlling the occupied territories. Slowly, he
believed, the million Arabs of these areas, one-third of all
those who consider themselves Palestinians, would recognize
that their interests lay in peace, trade, and good relations. He
was convinced that this view would spread to external Palestinians; "maybe it'll take a decade before we can negotiate."

In this official's analysis, though, the future would lie to a
large extent in the developing world, in Africa and Latin
America and even Asia. There, Israel had a great deal to
teach, great natural advantages. There were over twenty
Israeli missions in African countries and they produced
many orders for Israeli equipment. Moreover, Israel was
already building factories in two countries to start local
production of needed domestic products.

Sooner or later, the official reasoned, a double result
would eventuate. The less-developed nations would become
the best customers and reliable friends of Israel, and the
Western democracies would realize the advantage of Israel's
position as an intermediate country that could be of greatest
assistance as a sort of buffer-mediator. In fact, he said, U.S.
assistance programs were already contracting for Israeli
know-how.

Meanwhile, Israel could now afford to wait until Arab
states finally accepted the reality that Israel was ready to

negotiate a real peace at any time with any or all of her neighbors; Israeli leaders had said so over and over again. It could wait even longer for the Palestinian Arabs to come to terms with these realities; right now they were romantic and suicidal. In the end, Israel would deal with them fairly and try to resolve the hurt they had suffered—but here the West would finally need to recognize its responsibility. This, clearly, was long-range thinking based on a sense of confidence and security. The argument was so well constructed that it is difficult to label it as grandiose; nevertheless, the attitude of assured certainty did not accord with the actual position of a small nation with limited resources in a changing political world.

One of the more troubled conversations among Israelis during this period concerned the degree of colonization of occupied territories which should be undertaken. One member of the committee spent an evening discussing this subject with a group of lawyers and judges. As always in Israel the conversation was serious and partly centered on the state of the nation. One of them spoke about the prospect of building a vacation house near El Arish in the Sinai. All of the participants knew the terms of UN Resolution 242, which had been accepted by the Israeli government but not by Arab neighbor states as a basis for negotiation. They knew that the Sinai belonged to Egypt under the terms of that resolution. Nonetheless, the possibilities for Israeli development in the Sinai were considered very tempting indeed; after all, the land was virtually unoccupied. It was even argued that if it were shown by Israelis that the area had worth and could sustain an economy, this would show the Arabs what could be done, even if the territory might eventually be relinquished.

The term "eventually" then became important to the discussion; no one could foresee when the conditions of Resolution 242 might be satisfied. The problem was considered to be not Israel's, but that of the Arab states; it did not appear likely to the participants in this discussion that Egypt would be prepared for a decade or two to accept the permanent and secure presence of Israel in the occupied territories of the Sinai. Meanwhile, did not Israel have the duty to make use of the land? It had come under occupation, they felt, only because of Egyptian actions and any value gained would amount to fair reparation. Furthermore, development—especially of mineral and possibly oil resources—might make resource-starved Egypt covet the area and be more disposed toward being reasonable. The discussion clearly revealed a conflict between the impulse toward assertiveness and a counsel of prudence.

Not all Israelis were so restrained. We talked with members of religious groups who insisted that settlements should be established throughout the West Bank by ancient and biblically-recorded right, latter-day Israeli pioneers who believed it was sound policy to place new settlements in the Sinai so that it would provide a defensive buffer, as well as contribute to economic growth. Despite these urgings, the Knesset resisted such temptations and was criticized for it. Discussions with Israelis at this time were characterized by a sense of being in charge, of mastery; the decisions that were taken would be Israeli decisions. This was a source of satisfaction and well-being; Israel controlled her own fate.

The impact of the seventeen day war (1973)

The Middle East has a new way of dividing its history, a new emotional calendar: before and after the October 1973 War. The impact of this war was intensified for Israel by the following psychologically significant phenomena:

1. The attack on Israel occurred on Yom Kippur (The Day of Atonement), the holiest day of the Jewish religious calendar. This timing had the impact of increasing the feelings of Jews throughout the world that, "*We* Jews were at-

tacked by them (non-Jews)." It increased the split between
good and bad peoples and revived ageless Jewish feelings
and memories of attack and ostracism. Because the attack
occurred on Yom Kippur, the population of Israel and Jewry
of the world learned about the attack in the synagogues. This
intensified the personal impact of the news in quantity and
quality. Yom Kippur is that special day of the year when Jews
traditionally review their historical roots and their personal
histories. Religious Jews felt unified in their rage at the
desecration of the holiest day of the year with the many
non-religious Jews who, troubled by a sense of guilt over
non-observance, might well have felt "more Jewish" on this
particular occasion.

2. There were other symbolic events which increased the
impact. El Al, Israel's national airline, was the only carrier
which maintained its flights to Israel, bringing home the sons
and daughters of Israel—and other Jews—to defend the
land of their ancestors. The style of the operation (strict
security including fighter plane escorts, tanks at the depar-
ture terminals of the European ports of embarkation) enhanced the feeling of danger to Israel, indeed to all Jews,
from "them," the hostile non-Jewish outsiders.

3. The vulnerability of Israeli pilots. Because the lightning
victory of 1967 owed so much to the air force, Israeli pilots
had become national heroes. The psychological basis for the
"heroization" of Israeli pilots was determined not only by the
fact that the pilots protected Israel's cities from attack and
ensured the survival of the Israelis themselves, but also that
the accomplishments of the Israeli pilots helped to negate
anti-Semitic depictions of the cowardly Jew and erased the
caricature of the Ghetto Jew. The screening of Israeli pilots is
meticulously carried out. All Israelis know that only the fittest among them will pass the strenuous tests required to
become a pilot. That the Israeli pilots fell from the skies,
victims of electronic weaponry, made the emotional trauma

also intolerable. The effects of the Arab missiles were devas-
tating not only to the pilots, but to the nation's prior sense of
pride and mastery. The fact that this advanced weaponry was
fabricated and transported from the Soviet Union accen-
tuated the trauma, and the new hurt became intertwined
with the old ones.

Israel's emotional shift was prompt and obvious. Over-
confidence and a certain arrogance were replaced by grief,
protectiveness, and an increased sense of unity and extended
family. All soldiers became "our children." The extended
family feeling was most apparent in the attitudes displayed in
hospitals and in the radio messages from soldiers at the front
to their families. The intimate "shtetl"* atmosphere of endangered survival characteristic of Eastern European Jewish
ghetto life was reactivated.

Israeli attitudes toward the adversary showed surprising
flexibility, shifting rapidly from previously held views. The
Egyptians' technically skillful and swift crossing of the Suez
Canal altered the belief that the enemy was certain to blun-
der. The Israelis became extremely watchful. Initial
disbelief—"How could the disorganized Egyptian Army accomplish such a feat?"—gave way to serious self-questioning
about Israel's lack of preparation—"Why were our soldiers
caught in bathing suits at the Bar-Lev line?" Whereas the
Israelis had previously talked of Arab blunders, they now
talked about their *own*. They searched for failures in their
leadership, defense, and weaponry. They found it difficult to
face the most crucial psychological miscalculation: that they
had failed to see that their previous posture had stimulated
unity and determination among peoples of the surrounding
Arab states. Israeli over-confidence had blunted their perception of the social and military developments among the
Arabs. Israel did not appear to recognize that humiliating

* A Yiddish word meaning (an Eastern European) Jewish village.

memories, a sense of having been wronged, and international indifference can produce unity and determination in
another people, just as it had for the Israelis, and the modern
technology necessary to support their attempt to right perceived historical wrongs.

After the October 1973 War, Israelis had to realize that
their fate and existence were inextricably tied to the Middle
East and not Western Europe. Europe and the United States
were continuing their pursuit of material comforts (until the
oil blockade) while Israel was consumed in battle. Israelis
could not deny the Arab threat by pointing to the Arabs' lack
of unity, lack of modern equipment, or inability to coordinate their military strategy. In their hour of need, Israelis
were confronted with the stark realization that they depended on weapons and supplies from the United States.
Moshe Dayan conceded in a speech before the Knesset that
Israelis could no longer expect to call in Jewish aid on the
assumption that Jews everywhere "owed" Israel automatic
support in times of need. In 1973, the emergency airlift of
military supplies was loudly and clearly U.S. government aid.
The awareness of dependence was further altered by the
impact of the repeated diplomatic visits of Dr. Kissinger.
Since he was a Jew, many immigrant Jews were reminded of
their historical mistrust of Jews who had served foreign leaders. It reopened historical wounds of Jewish expulsion and of
homelessness. The 1973 War brought to the surface the
angry feelings of many Israelis toward those who had emigrated to Western countries, who accepted the interests of a
non-Jewish homeland as their own. The stance of dependence became increasingly intolerable. The stark perception
of reality, the hardship of a crippled economy, the shortages
in supplies that give enjoyment to everyday life, and an
inherent flexibility in the interest of survival moved Israelis
toward different preoccupations than their previous "show"
of independence. They gradually started to perceive the U.S.

Secretary of State as a representative of a changed reality rather than as the Jew who had left Germany before World War II.

Israel's relationship to the world community underwent a definite shift after the October War. Foes and friends declared themselves visibly and audibly. While Israelis at their radios listened with pounding hearts to the continual drone of the U.S. airlift, they also heard twenty African nations, prodded by Arab governments in the name of African solidarity, break diplomatic ties with them. Israel had once enjoyed good relations with 34 African nations, and Israeli collective farmers, teachers, and technicians had organized many successful development projects in Africa. Now even the nations that they had aided turned against them.*

The October War has also subtly—slowly, but perceptibly—influenced Israel's integration of European and Oriental Jews. The prism through which Israeli leaders of European background (Ashkenazim) and citizens had viewed Arabs in general had affected their view of their Oriental (Sephardic) population and their view of the Sephardim has affected their perception of the Arabs. They considered them incapable and "untalented" for modernization. The effective deployment of modern electronic weaponry by the Arabs during the October 1973 War altered some of these assumptions about Arabs and also "Ashkenazi" and "Sephardic" stereotypes. The "split" between Ashkenazim and Sephardim has been imperceptibly but subtly and favorably affected by the war.

During the October War the gap between old and new immigrants was bridged to some extent. The presence of these recent immigrants cushioned the feeling of being so outnumbered. It was remarkable that all Israelis interviewed

---

* Israelis insist that without their political conquests in Africa, Egyptians would not have agreed to negotiations because the Soviet Union only agreed to a cease fire after Israeli forces established a bridgehead in Egypt west of the Suez Canal.

in June 1973 had been preoccupied with their most recently arrived immigrants from the Soviet Union. In March 1974 Israelis did not speak of Soviet Jews. The only regular comment Israelis now made about Soviet Jewry was that they had given up trying to integrate the Georgian Jews.

Nothing had as profound an impact on Israelis as the loss of their sons, the more than 2,500 dead. They had wanted Israel for their children. They had wanted them to have what they had not had, a country to call their own; but suddenly they found themselves faced with having to sacrifice those for whom they wanted it all. The worry, the sorrow, and the heartbreak over losing their sons may influence child rearing practices in the next generation. It is impossible now for a mother of a young boy to avoid the thought that she might have to sacrifice him for the country. How this will alter the relationship of Israelis toward the institutions which create their soldiers (school, paramilitary, and the military, etc.) remains to be examined. "I love my country and my four little sons, and the two are incompatible," a young, intelligent and dedicated Israeli social worker told the interviewer.

Israelis as a people have experienced a deep narcissistic wound. In order to avoid and cushion some shifts in self-perception, Israelis engaged in assignment of blame toward their governmental and military leaders. Trust in this leadership decreased considerably in Israel in the months following the war. Israelis felt that their leaders had failed them, but that their sons had not. The leaders were accused of being outdated representatives of the past, and that their sons had fought against overwhelming odds. The turning point from an idolization of old leaders toward wholehearted care, nurturing, and feeling for the sons is a reflection of Israel's flexibility and continuing struggle for survival and mastery.

Young Israelis reappraised their leaders as well as their parents' dreams and aspirations. Detachment from the older generation is generating an increased cohesiveness among peers and an intense comradeship among the young. Whether this is a substitute for trust in leadership or whether this change can be utilized toward the development of mature participatory evaluation of external and internal realities remains to be seen.

The immediate response of many young Israelis was exemplified by the reaction of the eight Israeli students who were systematically interviewed in the United States in 1973 and summarized in the Appendix to this report. At the outset of the 1973 War, they were all immediately recalled to Israel. Several arrived in time to participate in the final rounds of battle. They all helped in the orderly civilian demobilization following the completion of cease-fire and truce negotiations. Then they returned to resume their studies. The feeling of certainty and confidence that they had manifested in these interviews right up to the outbreak of the War was markedly altered.

Initially, the returning Israelis were visibly subdued. Having anticipated a quick and total Israeli victory, all revealed the depression and cynicism that comes from the recognition of a wide gap between idealized-self and perceived-self. The arrogance evident prior to the October 1973 War had been replaced by a more quiet resolution. Evidence of narcissistic wounds was noticeable.

All political-military organizations have unique *narcissistically invested myths* rooted in actual historical events. The content of the myth usually is not current, but its loss is nonetheless a narcissistic injury. In 1967 Israeli pilots were believed to be nearly invincible, but they were not facing a Russian multi-tiered anti-aircraft missile system. In 1973 Israeli Air Force losses were high. As one Israeli student observed, "We lost a lot of planes (and pilots). Our guys (pilots) have skill and guts but the circumstances have changed. We didn't get the same results (as in 1967)." Another remarked, "We beat their armor but not like before—nothing like the old ratio." The outright derision of the Arab soldier's capabilities had vanished; a grudging respect for the Egyptian soldier by his Israeli counterpart had emerged. In fact, prior to October 1973, Israeli soldiers hardly believed that they really might have an Arab counterpart. This is no longer the case; times and realities have changed, person perception has changed, and inner representations have changed, accompanied by a predictable level of psychological distress. An Israeli offered the grudging compliment: "Who would have thought those guys could handle the bridging equipment (to cross the Suez Canal)?" The Egyptian Army had handled with skill Russian bridging equipment—a complicated operation for any army—and the Israeli Air Force had only temporarily been able to render useless two of the eleven bridges the Egyptians had put in place across the Canal.

Among Israeli civilians an emotional constriction and protectiveness was noted by these soldiers. "At home we became 'their children.'" Both soldiers and civilians blamed themselves and their government. "The Spartan life (of 1948, 1956, 1967 mythology and actuality) was lost" (between 1967–1973). "We should have known, we paid for it—3,000 dead," one student told the interviewer with bitter self-recrimination. These reflections were followed by an altered sense of political reality. "If we did it in two generations, it was arrogant of us to think that they (the Arabs) would take forever."

What do these psychological changes in Israelis portend for the future? If Israeli decision-makers were to experience these same psychological changes, two trends would emerge. To the extent that each side could engage in *narcissistic mirroring*, or reciprocity, or complementarity—each could perceive the other as a *significant* other.* Such an individual has

---

* This is one source of the total welcoming of President Sadat on his historic visit to Jerusalem in November, 1977, that has created another landmark date in the Arab-Israeli chronology.

earned the respect which one accords one's counterpart or opposite number. As one Israeli remarked, "Before 1973 we didn't think much of them but now they've earned the right to negotiate soldier-to-soldier (a reference to the cease-fire negotiations in the field at Suez)."

The second trend derives from a sense of increased vulnerability by the Israelis; not helplessness by any means, but vulnerability. In an attempt to offset vulnerability, young Israelis are giving some thought to the tactical use of nuclear weapons. "We'll never overcome their edge in manpower— but we do have the technology to go nuclear."

One Israeli, who had been present at the cease-fire negotiating site, remarked, "The Egyptians are not exactly our comrades-in-arms, and they are not fellow professionals who just happen to be on the other side—*but* I think of them as being a lot closer to that than I used to." This Israeli did not accord the same degree of respect to Syrian or Iraqi soldiers, nor to Palestinian guerrillas.

The respect accorded to Arab soldiers by Finnish officers of the UN Emergency Force was also crucial since both Arab and Israeli officers respect the Finnish military, based upon the legend and facts of Finland's military prowess in the Finnish war against the USSR during the winter of 1939.*

The Arab Palestinian problem

From the moment of the founding of Israel and the War of Independence, the relationship of the Jewish Israeli to Arab Palestinians, especially those who were incorporated into the population of the state, has presented a profound and continuing psychological problem for most Israelis. While there have been attitudinal shifts varying from marked ambivalence toward acceptance of separate but equal status, the

*This observation suggests that the choice of third party intermediaries must be attuned to these psychological dimensions. Certain third parties by reason of their perceived history might be better suited for this role than other candidates.

problem has often been resolved by denial of political claims to the point of what we have termed "narcissistic disacknowledgment." Here, we will report several vignettes of interviews and outline some of the psychological dynamics that seem to be involved. We will not review the political facets of relations between Israel and internal and external Palestinians.

The official policy was to treat the Arabs of Israel as citizens of the new state, but the areas in which most Palestine Arabs lived were declared security zones and placed under military governors while the people were subject to complex legal restrictions. Palestinian refugees outside the boundaries became wards of the United Nations or host countries and constantly clamored for repatriation and compensation for lost property. Despite numerous plans and missions, no substantial redress has been accomplished. It was in these circumstances that the people of Israel began to confront the problem of social integration of internal Palestinians and of international pressures emanating from refugees. These problems are still unresolved. Nonetheless, psychologically there has been some evidence of a gradual, though still limited, transformation from denial and disacknowledgement of the Palestinian claims to peoplehood toward recognition of otherness requiring acknowledgment and understanding in order to resolve relationships.

In the Israeli mind, there was a sharp distinction between internal Palestine Arabs and those living in other countries, but this attempt at distinction was frustrated by the knowledge that there was extensive communication and sense of connectedness between the separated communities. The fear that the Arab minority in Israel might act as a fifth column has never been resolved despite progress in integrating the minority into the social and political structure of the State. From the first, it was recognized that it would never be possible to persuade the Arab population to accept Israel's

firm commitment to being recognized as a "Jewish State" or
to accept its mission of the ingathering of the exiles. Israel's
solution has been to encourage separate Arab minority development, to gradually open channels of political expression, and to include some participation of Arab leaders in the
Israeli Knesset.

It is never forgotten in Israel that its government had
accepted the United Nations partition plan of 1947 and that
it was Arab neighbors who rejected the plan and attacked the
new state. In the Israeli view the responsibility for the plight
of Palestine Arab refugees therefore rests with the Arab
states and with the Palestinians. Therefore, it seemed only
logical and reasonable that these refugees should become
resettled in Arab countries, and with such compensation for
lost properties as could be equitably determined. A number
of attempts to arrange repatriation of at least some refugees
into Israel were made under the auspices of the UN's Palestine Conciliation Commission, but they all failed due to Israeli caution on the one hand and the refusal of Arab states
to make significant concessions in return. As time passed and
Palestine Arab border incidents grew in number and seriousness, and as Palestinian political organization appeared
and made claims to replace the Jewish State with a bi-national
secular state, the problem became frozen. Within Israel, disacknowledgment of external Palestinian Arab claims grew,
even as internal Arab minorities were cautiously brought into
the social and political life of the nation in a sort of troubled
co-existence within a common administrative structure.

Yet another shift has gradually taken place. At the political
level there was a virtual consensus among Israelis that the
real enemy of Israel at its inception and for the next twenty
years was Arab determination to destroy the new nation. It
was believed and argued that the Palestinian refugee problem was the product of manipulation by neighboring Arab
states, particularly by President Nasser of Egypt, who came

to be regarded as an Arab Hitler. After the Israeli victory in the 1967 War, this perception began to change. Before his death, Nasser came to be regarded within Israel as a possibly moderate national leader, while at the same time there was a striking shift toward regarding the PLO and its leader Yasir Arafat as the prime adversary. This attitudinal shift was significantly intensified by the 1973 War and subsequent negotiations. Nasser's successor, Anwar el-Sadat, has been perceived as a dangerous adversary who, however, could be dealt with without risk of humiliation, while the PLO and Arafat have been increasingly viewed as the major source of threat.

In terms of the psychology of self-involvement with the nation, it appears that two major dynamics are involved. The memory of the World War II Holocaust needed to be un-done, while at the same time it provided the rationale for extreme Israeli watchfulness against the threat of further injury and humiliation. Secondly, the merger of the self with the idealized nation required that the nation be established within distinct boundaries and even be polarized toward other nations. Rage and aggressive reactions to past and anticipated humiliation could be channelled toward depised outsiders.* Development of the capacity for understanding of and empathy for the Palestine Arabs and their purposes would reflect maturing of the collective self. It would reflect the beginnings of a transformation of shared self-involvements with the nation, from compensatory attempts to overcome personal and group injury to realistic affirmation of extended (national) selfhood which recognizes others while asserting its existence realistically.

It would be misleading to suggest that there is national unanimity in Israel in assessment of Arab minority relations.

---

* This view may have become substantially altered by President Sadat's dramatic visit to Jerusalem in November, 1977, and the subsequent face-to-face negotiating process between Israeli and Egyptian officials.

Scarcely any issue has been the subject of more vigorous and agonized debate at all levels, including non-official citizens. Throughout the history of the State there has been considerable strain between those agencies concerned with social development, such as the Ministry of Education, and those concerned with security and military affairs, a strain reflecting the continuing doubts of the degree of loyalty that could be expected of people who could never subscribe fully to the charter of the nation.

There has never been substantial question as to the minority status of Arabs in Israel; attention has been focused mainly on the treatment of this minority. For some time after the founding of Israel a small number of intellectuals and idealists advocated full bi-nationalism, equality of the Arab minority in the functions of the society in all respects. Leaders of the *Ihud* movement that advocated this policy referred one member of our committee to a man (Mr. Y) whom they believed exemplified the realistic possibilities in 1960, an Israeli government representative who performed liaison services with Arab minority communities and who was said to "completely understand and sympathize with" the people with whom he dealt.

Before the interviewer met Mr. Y, he visited an Arab village in Israel, and in the course of conversations introduced Mr. Y's name. The response was immediate, "Oh, him. He's Ben Gurion's Gestapo."

Mr. Y was indeed a charming and an intense man, deeply involved in the Arab minority problem. His knowledge was both intimate and encyclopedic; he had grown up on a small farm set in the midst of Arab people during the Mandate and his friends and schoolmates had been Arab neighbors. His Jewish education had been at home until he was 13 years old. He had then been sent to Hebrew-speaking schools in the nearest town, forty miles away from home. He remembered well the sense of loss at separation from his friends and always renewed these relationships during the school holidays. He had, as a matter of course, fought in the War of Independence but he never regarded the Arabs of Palestine as his enemies. As he said, "They didn't fight us. We didn't fight them. It was entirely a battle with outsiders, people who had nothing to do with Palestine or with Israel. They were vying for power and for dominance in the Arab world; they didn't care a bit about Palestine or about Palestinians. They deserved to be defeated—and they were."

Mr. Y, who was then in his early twenties, immediately began his career as a mediator between Palestine Arabs and the Israeli government; such knowledge and talents as his were rare and needed. His position was difficult. He was a loyal and proud Israeli but his assigned task involved interpreting the sentiments and needs of the Arab minority to an unreceptive and security-conscious Israeli government and bureaucracy while simultaneously defending the decisions of the government to the leaders of the Arab communities in such a way as to make them maximally acceptable. Despite the intrinsic paradoxes of this position he relished the task. He had worked unremittingly for a dozen years at it. His skills were impressive. He could, with equal facility, make cases for each side on nearly any issue. Foremost at the time of the interview were further forced acquisitions of Arab lands by the Israeli government on grounds of security needs.

In general, Mr. Y, although he was cautious, was extremely critical of his government's minority policies. He believed, in the first place, that there had been no clear policy in the twelve years of Israel's existence; rather, there had been vacillation, confusion, and inconsistency. What was needed above all, he thought, was firmness, fairness, and strength. The Arab minorities of Israel needed to know where they stood, what they could expect. If that were the case, they would certainly complain—because they always complained—

but they would become Israeli Arabs instead of Palestinian Arabs. As it was, they were only encouraged to emphasize their separateness, their disloyalty to the state. They got more concessions from the government that way. Besides, he believed, the government of Israel had not been fair to the Arab minority, especially with respect to land tenure. Government officials simply did not understand the attachment of the Arab farmer or villager to his particular land and home. Many tracts of land were co-opted by the State and left lying untilled; many of the Arab minority were taken from their homes and resettled arbitrarily. It appeared to the Arab minority that there was a deliberate effort to destroy their sense of community and their traditional way of life. Mr. Y understood the Israeli mind and reasoning for each of its steps, but he could not forgive its insensitivity to the people whose cause it was his task to represent.

When he spoke of the Arab minority, Mr. Y was at first most cautious and advocated only firm handling. But as the discussion progressed over time, he became more and more emphatic; Arabs were like children. They would behave only so long as they knew they were being watched; they could not be trusted. As a matter of fact, he thought, the Israeli government overestimated the capacity of the Arab minority to organize and to act. They were not like European Jews. In fact, their needs were simple, and if these were met they would be content and even willing subjects. It was too bad that the complainers had such effect; the Palestine Arabs had complained for centuries even as they accepted the dominance of successive authorities. Why should that change now?

Mr. Y believed that he had more Arab than Jewish friends, that is, people whom he could rely on to be responsive, people who could be flexible and accommodating, with whom it was much easier to deal than with most Israelis. He was almost scornful of the fear of the Arab minority that he found prevalent. He said, "If you understand them, there's nothing to be afraid of at all. They aren't dangerous because they aren't very brave; they don't fight for their cause. They only talk. You have to watch them, of course, and you have to let them know that they can't get away with anything, but if you do that they can be good friends, very helpful." The interviewer remarked that his attitude seemed a bit like that of Americans toward its native Indians, that the Arabs were charges to be looked after but not to be accorded full equality.

To the interviewer's surprise, Mr. Y agreed. "That's exactly right. They can be treated with respect but they will never be loyal. They are outsiders and that's what they want to be. If they are treated correctly they can be useful, they can be examples; the rest of the Arab world can't complain because they will actually be better off than before and better off than other Arabs. As long as that is true they will behave. They won't endanger their advantages. But they must be treated correctly." It was then that Mr. Y described the critical event of his life.

When he was twelve years old, his father was shot from long range as he worked his fields. The boy was certain of the source of the attack, a nearby Arab village where some of his friends lived. Its people had been stirred by Zionist incursions. He took his father's rifle that night and crept to a little hill above the village. Just as he had the village leader in the cross-hairs of his telescopic sight, a woman whom he knew crossed his field of fire, an infant at her breast. He was paralyzed, held his fire, and he realized that his Arab neighbors were "human beings with troubles." He never forgave the murder of his father, but from that moment on devoted himself to the "civilizing" of the Arab people.

Having recounted this incident, Mr. Y's commitments could be more clearly understood. Arabs, to him, represented a primitive group to be mastered, to be controlled.

Although he had seen them as human beings, he did not and never would accept them as "civilized," as worthy members of his group, his nation. His disagreement with government policies was not based on a commitment to Arab equality or full participation in the administration of the nation, but rather was concerned with their management, how they should be treated so as to ensure their cooperative behavior. But he explicitly rejected elements of violence and rebellion. No part of Mr. Y's selfhood was identified with his Arab friends.

The interviewer was shocked; he had shared the hopes of his *Ihud* sponsors that a genuine rapprochement might be possible. In a subsequent discussion with them, they admitted the problem, the powerful pull of ethnic and historic identity; the practical and psychological difficulty, if not impossibility, of creating a common nation from such disparate senses of self. The extended "I" could not transcend the opposite "Other." A political ideal seemed less and less possible to achieve.

In fact, less dramatic examples of the polarization of group selfhood abounded in Israel and have been reinforced by every Arab revolt, protest, attack, or act of terror. Nearly every Israeli has been personally touched by the death or injury of some relative or friend by Arab or Palestinian acts of terrorism. Experiences of this kind have solidified the cohesiveness of the extended Jewish Israeli self and intensified the exclusion of Arabs from within the boundaries of true national membership. On the other hand, there has been movement toward acceptance of Israel's Arab minority among some elements of Israeli society.

A poignant example of early childhood learning about the negative stereotyping of the Arab people was recounted to one member of our committee by an Israeli psychologist who provided services to a new Israeli town below the Golan Heights, from which occasional shellings and shootings had emanated. The townspeople kept guns at the ready and had armored their tractors. The psychologist had play therapy materials, among which was a doll in Arab costume. When the interviewer asked how children used this doll, he was told, "Oh, that is the bad doll. The children have it do all the bad things that they would like to do but aren't allowed to. It steals and peeks and even hurts or kills anyone the child is angry at." The psychologist went on sadly to deplore the very early formation of such hostile images; "After all, there are Arab settlements only a kilometer away from here, but by as early as 2½ years our children are already convinced that the Arab people are quite impossible—our children avoid all real contact with them."

The Six-Day War of 1967 significantly changed the relationship between Israeli and Palestinian Arab. There was very little agitation by the Arab minority of Israel and certainly no "fifth column" kind of activity. Palestine Arabs living on the West Bank and Gaza areas for the most part avoided any contact with Israeli troops. Furthermore, policies that allowed visits of the Arab people of the Administered Regions to their former homes and friends led to a sympathetic realization of the reality of the Arab people's displacement. Stories were told repeatedly of Arab and Jewish families weeping together over the tragedy of Jewish occupation of Arab homes and land. Finally, Israeli euphoria following the lightning victories of that war allowed a sense of security and mastery for the first time since Israel's founding 19 years earlier. Israelis were suddenly less fearful of Arab threat from without or within. As a result, the policies of administration were clear-cut and firm, and were quite flexible with respect to Arabs' travel and freedom of expression. The Israeli "self" and Arab "other" acknowledged each other as alien and different, but some Israelis felt less threatened by the Arabs among them.

In 1960, when the interviews reported above were carried out, there were relatively few Israeli specialists on Arab life and culture, and almost all of these approached their subjects as *objects* of scholarship or practical administration. Expertise was of a high order but thinly spread; our discussions with experts found knowledge without empathy. A decade later, in 1970, there was increased Israeli contact, knowledge, and concern.

An old acquaintance of one of the committee members, a person who specialized in the export of development technology to other countries to the considerable profit of Israel, was eager to illustrate the changed psychological climate. This seemed all the more remarkable as his son had been killed in the 1967 War and was still mourned. Mr. N commented, "We can't survive on enmity. We must work with other people as people, different from ourselves, certainly, but entitled to their own lives and ways of life, just as we are entitled to ours. It's time we learned that and we are learning it. I think my son might be alive today if we had been able—had been allowed by our circumstances—to come to grips with the problems our neighbors face. Now, since 1967, we can begin to do that. I'd like to think that my son did not die in vain for his country." He then proposed an evening's discussion with some of the "new Israeli men," men who were at work on reconciliation of Israel with her Arab minorities and Arab neighbors.

The group of eight men and women whom he invited came from universities, the government, and administration. One was a teacher of Arab culture in a Hebrew grammar school. Discussion was intense and animated. The group agreed that theirs were minority attitudes, listened to but not supported by high level government officials. What was remarkable was the degree to which they were able to articulate the Arab case, of both internal and external Palestinian

Arabs. A number of policies were reviewed from the Arab point of view; some were criticized from the standpoint of Israel's self interest.

When the interviewer related some of the observations reported above, most of the group members agreed that they had themselves shared the outlook of fear and treating-as-objects toward the Arab people a decade before; their attitudes had undergone a transformation in the decade—this change included experienced scholars of the Arab world. The change could be characterized as the emergence of empathy, the humanization of the other. In fact, the process had gone much further. Empathic appreciation of the other was being advocated by an articulate, though still small, intellectual minority of Israelis, of whom those present were representative.

In an effort to understand this attitudinal shift, we have hypothesized that this small group of individuals had become secure in their extended, national selfhood, so secure as to be unthreatened by otherness. This had not decreased their commitment to live, work, or fight for Israel. However, they could tolerate and then accept the recognition of others without threat to the coherence of their sense of self. These Israelis gained real satisfaction from exchanges of recognition, however long distance, with Arab peoples. This new-found capacity to recognize complex psychological motives and configurations of the Arab mind and culture greatly enhanced their ability to predict Arab behavior and response. They became less anxious in their relationships with Arabs because of their ability to understand them better. It is not possible to determine how widespread this increased recognition of the Arab other is among Israelis, how influential this minority may become, how firmly it could resist regression in the face of continued conflict. It is noteworthy, though, that after the 1973 War, despite retrenchment of some Israeli policy positions, there nonetheless has been increased progress toward face-to-face negotiations between Arabs and Israelis.

Dynamics of Israeli self-involvement

A tentative model of the evolution of Israeli extended self-involvement with the nation can be attempted in terms of the modal configuration of group narcissism. As hypothesized in Chapter 2, the investment of extended self interest in the nation leads to common dynamic responses of individuals to the impingement of external events on the nation which are experienced as though they directly affected the person. Great and threatening events, especially war, mobilize such reactions to such a degree and among such a high proportion of the people that it seems justified to consider group narcissistic reactions as contributive to national perception, behavior, and policy formation.

The preliminary model that we have constructed is based on an interpretation of the observations reported in this Chapter and Appendix, and drawn directly from Israelis interviewed by members of our committee. Our reliance on direct observations prevents us from extending the model to the long history of Jewish peoplehood, but must begin with the living memories of our subjects. It must be added, however, that the cultural history of the Jewish people is an integral part of our subjects' lives and is clearly interwoven with contemporary experience.

The founders of the Jewish national state had well-established concepts of nationhood, but mass mobilization to the idea did not occur until massive trauma to the group threatened both personal and group survival. In this circumstance the establishment of the state of Israel almost immediately produced a sense of intense inter-relatedness of self and country, a narcissistic hypercathexis marked by merger of the nation with the extended self. Subsequent participa-

Chronology of Historic Events and Their Effects on Politics and Personality

Historic Event	Extended-Self Configuration	Political Object Relations
Exile (135–1948 C.E.) Pogroms to the Holocaust, Zionism	Massive trauma and humiliation, refugeeism, political mobilization	Ambivalence but growth of demand for autonomy, a "homeland"
Proclamation of State War of Independence 1948–1949	Self-object merger with nation, heroic idealizing in action (nation building)	Survival followed by self-absorption
Sinai War, a policy war—1956	Rage at previous humiliation, continuing threat focused on "enemy"	Preoccupation to eliminate enemy (Nasser)
June War—1967	Revival of vulnerability feelings followed by merger with grandiose self-extension (super-man and unrealistic autonomy, "never again)"	Aggrandizement and disacknowledgment, "We don't need anybody," narcissistic isolation
October War, defense of the nation—1973	Temporary fragmentation followed by intense mirroring with adversaries and supporters. Gradual reorganization toward self-object differentiation	Forced confrontation followed by rapid acknowledgment of Egypt; some mutual mirroring; gradual adversary recognition of Arab neighbors. Painful awareness of limits on autonomy

tion in national life mobilized dynamic reactions of the self system to a degree that profoundly affected personal and national self-esteem. At this point we can outline what appear to be shared reactions to major events befalling the nation. Since the construct is abstracted from a substantial mass of data reinterpreted in terms of the hypothesis of self-involvement in nation, we have not felt justified in linking the stages directly to case studies, especially since we are aware of both precedents and exceptions for each configuration that we have posited.

Comparison of emerging themes of Israeli and Palestinian political self-development suggests some tendency toward development and consolidation of realistic self-esteem with diminishing needs to deny or disacknowledge the claims of others—at least through 1974. This development is further advanced in the case of the Israeli group self in terms of the history of the spread of the sense of nation idea and the political-juridical development of the State. This represents a hopeful factor for the eventual resolution of the conflict which appears to have been fueled perhaps as much by psychological forces as by power realities. In terms of the hypothesis we have proposed, "narcissistic disacknowledgment" may be diminishing, and some degree of "mirroring" may have begun to take place.

References

1. A. Elon. THE ISRAELIS: FOUNDERS AND SONS (New York: Holt, Rinehart and Winston, 1971).
2. Rita R. Rogers. The Emotional Climate in Israeli Society, *American Journal of Psychiatry* 128, 8 (1972) 988–992.
3. Ibid.
4. Ibid.
5. Ibid.

5

EXTENDED SELF AND INTERNATIONAL RELATIONS: SOME IMPLICATIONS AND SPECULATIONS

The International Relations Committee of GAP has long been interested in the psychology of man's participation in war. The familiar explanations: instinctual aggression, Skinnerian conditioning, frustration-aggression, and individual psychopathology, have not been compelling. They are at best only partial explanations. The universal willingness of people to do things in war which they wouldn't do as individuals, to kill and to expose themselves to being killed for instance, appears to us to call for psychological explanations which fit with universal psychological developmental themes.

In recent years members of the committee have studied in several countries the engagement of individuals and ethnic groups in the Middle East conflict. While these observations were being discussed within the committee, concurrent psychoanalytic considerations based on clinical experience showed a remarkable convergence of studies of war participation behavior and work on individual narcissism by Kohut, Rochlin and Kernberg.* It appeared to us that Kohut's analysis of problems of patients who suffer from narcissistic difficulties showed a considerable similarity to the psychological organization of subjects we interviewed about their roles in the protracted Arab-Israeli conflict.

Kohut extended earlier conceptions of narcissism (the investment of psychological libido or energy in the self) and proposed that it has a line or course of development separate

---

* See references in Chapter 1 by these authors.

559

from the familiar psychosexual line of development. This line of growth is central to the evolution of the self.

In Chapter 2 while tracing the development of a sense of self in the individual, we noted the narcissistic matrix of continuity with mother from which the self gradually separates. The self's proclivity to experience elements of its outer world, personal, social, and inanimate, as integral parts of itself is drawn from this matrix. People come to regard their fellow citizens, cities and country, symbols such as the flag, language, culture, etc., as part of the self, an extended self. Danger to these extensions of the self may be experienced as dangers to the self. National crises activate the extended-self system with consequent hypercathexis of its extensive set of self-objects. Experiences mutually shared with and validated by fellow citizens reinforce the extended self system providing a powerful emotional climate for the development and pursuit of particular national policies.

The narcissistic core of the self is susceptible to enhancement and threat from without as well as from internal processes of psychopathology. Kohut observed that responses to narcissistic injury include severe rage, quest for vengeance, ostracism, intense demand for attention, and the need for merger with idealized and omnipotent parent imagos. The application of these clinical insights makes more understandable a number of widely shared reactions of participants in the Middle East conflict, such as: the implacable rage of the Palestinians in response to political humiliation; acts of terrorism against civilians; the exaggerated self-confidence of Israelis after the triumph of the 1967 War; Egyptian pride disproportionate to their limited Suez success in the war of 1973. These highly personal but widely experienced psychological reactions may be seen as co-determinants of national behavior and policy, along with political realities; for example, the increasing psychological capacity of Egyptians to accept Israel's existence, and Israel's neglect of intelligence reports on the eve of the 1973 War. We believe that peoples in conflict show signs of proceeding in their psychological development from reliance on mutual denial and ostracism to positive processes of mutual mirroring.

Implications; psychology of group participation

At first glance, it would seem to be obvious that people will go to war in order to preserve or add to their vital interests and protect themselves. However, the definition of vital interests and threat to survival varies both individually and culturally. Threats may be perceived to be real and vital at one historical moment, but merely bluff at another time. Because these differences in evaluating risk and threat are determined by differences in interpretation of events and response to them, this committee is persuaded that psychology has a significant contribution to make in the analysis and understanding of international relations. William Harvey knew, as generations before him knew, that blood flows, but he recognized the importance of extending this commonplace observation by scientific study of the blood's "exercitatio" or dynamics. Our work entails the simultaneous observation and analysis of individual psychodynamics in interaction with national behavior in making war, as well as some psychological aspects of relations between nations. This is a major step for psychiatrists who have generally been restrained by the caveat to "stick to their knitting" and confine their analysis to individual behavior—to deviant or disordered forms of behavior. But the impact of social events on the person and personal involvement in those events is a matter of increasing general, as well as professional, interest. The present study manifests this interest, focusing on the critical social phenomenon of war. We are struck by the lack of an established body of theory dealing with the psychological and behavioral linkages between the individual and society.

In the body of this report we have confined ourselves to formulating a hypothesis and applying it to a specific case study. In this final chapter we will consider some implications of the hypothesis for the broader dynamics of international relations. In our committee work we developed the feeling that we have a tenuous hold on a powerful set of ideas which may illuminate the political process not only in relation to war, but wherever people are involved in political behavior. We recognize the need both to define and to refine this tool and to examine related hypotheses. This chapter attempts to anticipate some of these issues; we do so with the conviction that in this field there are no sorcerers—only apprentices.

The engagement of psychiatrists in the field of international relations is part of a historical evolution which contains some pertinent parallelisms. Just as Renaissance physicians had to shake off the lethargy and prejudices of the dark ages to recommence the study of anatomy, physicians of the 19th century had to overcome obstacles in bringing themselves to the systematic study of abnormal behavior. The application of physics and chemistry to medicine had given the profession a new scientific legitimacy which tended to strengthen the explanatory focus on organic factors in illness as contrasted with psychological factors. Initially, as with anatomy, the study of psychiatry was descriptive and static. Numerous clinicians independently delineated syndromes and mental illnesses, but the patient was ever viewed in isolation, and the illness as having a course but no dynamics.

When Freud elaborated a dynamic concept of mental life, he left it rooted in biological or instinctual processes. Contemporary psychiatry, while retaining much of its Freudian base, has been increasingly concerned with the impact of the family and social factors on individual psychological development. This in turn has led to a more careful study of the wider circles of family and other social groups to which individuals belong. As we have studied such groups (often having artificially created them as in group therapy), we have been struck by a whole body of psychodynamics which occurs, not only between members of the group but in the group as a unit, and finally as it interacts with other groups. As noted earlier, we are extremely cautious about extrapolating from individual psychology to group psychology, and especially so as the groups grow larger and merge together as societies and nations. Nevertheless, there are parallels as well as differences which must be defined if we are to avoid the error of studying the behavior of nations as though it lacks a human ingredient.

A significant source of differences between individual and group behavior lies in their development. Individual development, physical and psychological, occurs in a strict sequence of stages, with each succeeding one building on those which have gone before. Concept formation cannot occur until the child has mastered perception, apperception, concrete thinking, and so forth. The epigenetic or life cycle principle of personality development is generally accepted in psychology, although various interpretations or modifications of the principle are offered by different schools of thought. Examination of group development reveals it to be much less regular, and in certain respects more complex. It does not occur in a strictly epigenetic manner, although it can be seen that there are certain developmental tasks characteristic of all groups, such as the establishment of boundaries, acceptable membership, and the development of purposes and cohesiveness.

Individual behavior which can be identified as regressed or fixated at certain developmental stages does not have a strict analogue in group behavior, perhaps because most groups contain certain relatively unconflicted members who are capable of getting the group "unstuck" and advancing its development. Nonetheless, some groups may, at least temporarily, manifest behavior which is inappropriate or irrational, often as a result of the temporary ascendancy of certain members or of processes such as conflict, dominance, or rebellion. Such group responses occur, not only in relation to constantly fluctuating interactions of the personalities of the members, but also in response to external influences. The resultant behavior occurring in both directions along a progression-regression axis often bears a striking resemblance to the vicissitudes of individual development, and may even reflect the character stamp of a single member.

Depending upon the mix of its membership and their attributes, groups develop a certain identity or character which in a nation-sized group contributes to the "national character" concept. When individual behavior is extensively influenced by the established identity and tends to be in a high degree predictable, the behavior is said to be "in character." To a lesser extent, but still significantly, "national behavior" tends to move in accordance with a collective sense of the conscious and unconscious identity which a people share and in a sense cannot escape. A pooled common denominator of psychological experience may explain certain elements of national behavior and constitute part of the psychodynamic core of the interaction of man and nation.

Violent manifestations of narcissistic rage occur rarely in the repertoire of individual behavior. An ingrained sense of values and fear of punishment restrain the murderous impulses. It is a paradox that nations and factions within them perform murderous acts—sometimes on a vast scale. The decision-making group usually has a great deal of time for contemplation and includes members of mature personality who might be expected to moderate the impulsive members. And no doubt many times they do; but we must account for the frequency of failure to do so. We recognize, of course, the reasoned use of war to advance national policy. Psychiatric experience repeatedly confirms that individual acts of violence are at their most heinous not in "wild" outbursts but in states of narcissistic rage where, as Kohut points out, the intellect makes possible the organized efficiency necessary for making war.

The Committee on Social Issues of GAP, in a report published in 1964 entitled PSYCHIATRIC ASPECTS OF THE PREVENTION OF NUCLEAR WAR,[1] discussed some subjects germane to our current theme; some review will be helpful. The report identified the psychological process of "dehumanization" as a prerequisite to people's ability to tolerate mass destruction and recognized two separate (though related) components in it: object-directed dehumanization and self-directed dehumanization.

Object-directed dehumanization diminishes the other by denying him some of the attributes of humans. By implying that he is non-human he may therefore be dealt with as a lower animal species. In another form, this process treats people as statistics, as items of consumable supply. The psychological mechanisms employed in making numbers out of people work a subtle erosion of the person's self image. Blocking off a whole constellation of feelings of fear, compassion, guilt and shame reduces the capacity to feel, and so to act, as a full human being. One may become simply "a cog in the machine" which is only "following orders." As a result, the ability to identify with others is impaired and one loses qualities of autonomy, courage, and responsibility.

The adaptive utility of a degree of object-dehumanization is recognized. In the normal care of the sick and especially in times of such major calamities as war, epidemics and natural disasters, psychic mechanisms against pity, terror, and disgust are necessary to accomplish the work of mercy. In our complex and often impersonal society, the increased emotional distance from others, diminished sense of personal responsibility for the consequences of one's actions, inability to oppose dominant group pressures, and feelings of personal helplessness predispose us to maladaptive and regressive dehumanization.

While the present work has shown how man invests his surrounding world, including its inanimate parts,* with a sense of himself to conceive of it as an extension of his self, and is therefore willing to fight for it as for his life, the earlier GAP report demonstrates how the psychological process of dehumanization enables man, by a psychological commutation, to divest the enemy not only of his surrounding world, but of his very life. This entails a suspension of pity requiring an alteration of conscience. Traditionally, conscience is thought of as fixed, both as a quality of the individual and as a social ethic. The formulation of extended self suggests that "others" or "not-self" are exempted from the social ethic. Studies of group behavior have repeatedly demonstrated the malleability of conscience. Psychological experiments, one of which is cited in the earlier GAP report, have shown how individuals succumb to group pressures and distant or impersonal relations with others in such a way as to distort perception and judgment and even to engage in unwanted acts of sadism.

The effectiveness of group therapy is based in part on moderating the superego by the empathic attitudes of individuals and of the group as a whole. Under the stress of war, and especially in battle conditions, atrocities become possible partly because of the synergistic tolerance of those with whom the murderous soldier is in immediate contact. War offers all too much evidence of the inefficiency of the pliable conscience in protecting us from our baser selves. Morality is immutable mainly in the preached ideal and in myth; the myth seems to know its own weakness and so claims to be graven in stone.

* See Appendix.

Group therapy movement on the progression-regression axis is often most evident in periods of crisis; and again analogously the same appears to be true of national life where the crises of war, economic depression, etc., mobilize and unify people's feelings and efforts into a national mood, will, and course of responsible, constructive action. However, there are exceptions, especially when a people's cohesion and continuity are felt to be threatened.

Some speculative applications

The Treaty of Versailles, with its strictures on German economy and power, was experienced with such unanimity by the German people as a hopeless humiliation of a deeply personal nature that it can be understood to have constituted a national psychological trauma. Although the immediate impact of the treaty was fragmenting in political terms, it was soon to prove a unifying experience which may have contributed to the regressive behavior of a whole people's merger with Hitler as the personification of an omnipotent and idealized self-object promising to avenge the people's narcissistic injury. The conditions of the Treaty may have been experienced as a symbolic continuation of the international and inter-ethnic murder of World War I and so may have added impetus to German vengeance, which in the war that resumed in 1939–45, resulted in the slaughter of a helpless ethnic group, the Jews.

The subsequent dynamic reaction by the survivors of that group gave birth to the modern nation-state of Israel, a development that can be conceptualized from one psychological perspective as a creative employment of injured narcissism. But the creation of the state of Israel rendered many Palestinians homeless and evoked in them a determination to right the wrong they have suffered. We find in this chain of events an instance of the apparent psychological continuity of history. We consider this factor to rank with power politics and economics as one of the powerful determinants of human history.

Some of the dynamics under discussion may be represented in the recent history of the U.S. Assuming free world leadership after World War II may have induced an identity crisis of sorts. Among the many psychological traits which asserted themselves alternately and simultaneously was the dichotomy of an open liberality and an old fixation in Puritan demand for righteous behavior. The unconscious personification function which leaders play found some capable actors in the benevolent parent image of Eisenhower and that Crusader's choice of Secretary of State, John Foster Dulles, who represented a broadly supported though unconscious need for moral conformity. There came to ascendancy in policy a militant anticommunism which was not satisfied with a degree of moral imperialism which found neutralism sinful, but finally erupted in the punitive violence of Southeast Asia.

The emergence of many new nations in the past 20 years has proceeded in a relatively peaceful manner, but there are numerous instances of tormented periods of national life in which particular leaders or factions not only engage in power grabs, but seek to mold their nation's life and character into that of an obedient self-object, as Nkrumah may have done in Ghana. Some of this behavior is relatively harmless, but some of it is internationally dangerous and self-destructive. Rational values are swept aside by considerations which are largely unconsciously powered in spite of the political rationalizations offered.

The positions of the Israeli and Palestinian peoples in early stages of their political development made them psychologically vulnerable in their sense of identity. As we have pointed out in this report, some of the historical preconditions for the development of a healthy self-esteem and mature identity seem to have been jeopardized in both cases. True, the West in the past paid Israel an extravagant, albeit guilty, admiration, but this is now being moderated under the pressure of oil economics and politics. The neglect of the Palestinians by most nations is now being corrected by a sudden access of approval by the Arab World and beyond. In their formal and rhetorical postures, the Israelis and the Palestinians as peoples have treated each other with such total narcissistic disacknowledgment as to deny the other's existence or right to exist, though in practice they have been more "realistic" and have recognized that there was something to be destroyed.

The protracted lack of adequate mirroring from others left both Israelis and Palestinians little choice but to live within circumscribed systems of self-sustaining myths and historical convictions, while the absence of friendly, external, corrective views resulted in an intensification of ethnocentric identification. Limited outside contacts by both sides have often been used in the client-patron relationship to persuade the patron into the role of a compliant self-object whose function is to offer only favorable mirroring.

Discussion of this subject led the Committee to consider the relevance of Kohut's types of narcissistic transferences to furthering our understanding of national behavior. Narcissism is familiar as a quality of individuals, but there is a considerable conceptual shift in viewing it as a property of nations. However, our experience with groups suggests that a particular emotional reaction may be elicited among group members so broadly as to constitute the crucial mood and determinant of action. Mob violence, for example, is so universally feared as to suggest that individual violence is augmented by the group context. Such reactions are elicited not only by events which impinge on the group, but are often precipitated by dominant members, generally those with the greatest narcissistic needs. That these charismatic leaders are successful seems to stem from the energizing source of narcissism which is capable of moderating and pacifying, as well as inciting their followers to violent action. Widely shared social aspirations demand various expressions, including representation by leaders, a process known as the personification function. Such leaders then become objects of partial identification for their constituents, which in the dialectic process enables focusing and concretizing of social objectives.

Although individual narcissism was delineated in the context of psychoanalytic treatment, where it finds expression in the subject's transference behavior toward the analyst, it manifests itself in interpersonal relations. Three varieties have been described: mirroring, twin, and merger types. It appears to us that similar phenomena occur in groups and nations; here we will suggest how such group-transference behavior may be manifested in international relations.

At the national level it appears that narcissistic transference behavior of the narrow mirroring type might be responsible for leading a nation to seek approval on the basis of similarities of an ethnic or religious type in the client-patron relationship, as exemplified by Israel's appeal to the U.S. Transference of the twin or merger type appear to be relatively rare. But in times of real and intense emotional crisis, some Arab nations have called for merger with others. The restraint of Egypt in the face of Libya's demand for merger may testify, not only to the questionable political motives, but also to the impractical and regressive nature of the appeal in contrast to a more mature and rational integrative development. The surrender of sovereignty and of selfhood which would be implied in national behavior of a merger or twin type is usually resisted by the complexity of the national structure, and particularly by the inevitable presence of independent components within it.

The search for mirroring approval is not confined to allies, but ironically is also intensely sought from the enemy—and not always covertly. Demands are made at every level from international organizations to private musing about one's "opposite number." The projection of one's self into the other man's place is not done solely to figure him out and beat him—useful as this may be—but appears to stem from strong unconscious needs for recognition of one's person and role by important others, no matter how remote they may be emotionally or geographically. Innocent enhancement of narcissism works slowly and indirectly, but it works well. The respect accorded to the Egyptian military by their Israeli counterparts across all ranks after October 1973 can be productive of positive mutuality, in contrast to the inevitably destructive mutuality of narcissistic disacknowledgement.

Individual participation in mass aggression has its most vivid epiphany in terrorism. Here the action's component of narcissistic rage has been most compellingly evident in interviews with terrorists. Kohut describes some features of such rage: "Narcissistic rage occurs in many forms; they all share, however, a specific psychological flavor which gives them a distinct position within the wide realm of human aggressions. The need for revenge, for righting a wrong, for undoing a hurt by whatever means, and a deeply anchored, unrelenting compulsion in the pursuit of all these aims which gives no rest to those who have suffered a narcissistic injury—these are features which are characteristic for the phenomenon of narcissistic rage in all its forms and which set it apart from other kinds of aggression."[2]

We have observed that such men have an intense conviction that they are carrying out the will of a superior power—that they are acting on behalf of their country, or of God—in whose prerogatives they share. Their fanaticism is proverbially blind and lacking in empathy, but it is buttressed by rationalization, giving it at times a distinctly paranoid quality. Typically, the self-system of fanatics is controlled by fusion with the omnipotent self-object whether it be nation, ideology or God. The terrorist draws some of his fearless attitude toward death from this identification with the omnipotent self-object which will, in fact, survive his death. The provenant group perhaps discharges its debt and sustains the process by keeping alive the names of such "heroes." Kohut has also found that the narcissistically injured individual comparing himself with a successful rival feels an increased sense of shame and intense envy which may lead, not only to other-directed destruction, but also to suicidal behavior as the suffering ego struggles to wipe out the reality of failure by doing away with the self.

National states find it politically expedient and morally comforting to treat terrorism as criminal behavior and, when they can do so, tend to respond with unusual force (it is not in any way to condone terrorism to point out parenthetically that this often inspires a new cycle of terrorism). Massive force may deter such behavior to a certain extent as in the reprisal policies of the Nazis in occupied countries. But recent world history shows a certain revulsion from such measures. Within Israel a considerable body of opinion opposes massive reprisals. There are those who remember the desperation which drove some Jews to undertake acts of terrorism prior to the termination of the British Mandate in 1948. Coping with terrorism will require a more objective understanding of its psychological and political origins. We are struck by the exhibitionistic component, dramatic occasions and victims and demands for media exposure, which is completely consistent with the grandiose exhibitionistic nature of the narcissistic process. Some of the most successful handling of the hostage-taking type of terrorist behavior has been based on the psychological principle of patient restraint of intervention, while captors and captives discover their own and others' humanity in a strange sort of group encounter experience.

Dealing with terrorism requires careful identification of its motivation. Occasionally, acts of terrorism are the products of psychotic persons, psychopaths or criminals, but most terrorism is inspired by social, political or religious ideology. The ideology is sometimes difficult to recognize because it is inchoate, poorly articulated or has some radically new or different features. Some student terrorism on the contemporary European scene is of this hard-to-identify variety. It is vitally important to overcome psychological resistance, both individual and societal, to recognizing the ideology. A policy is being pursued and supported, at least by a minority, and so constitutes a significant part of national life. It cannot safely be dismissed as "insane criminal behavior," because, however mistakenly, people who are driven by an ideology will, unless their ideology is taken seriously, remain mobilized for and demand the expression of narcissistic rage. Equally, it must be realized that giving this kind of recognition in no way constitutes approval or agreement with that ideology.

Man's violent acts, whether performed solitarily or collectively, often appear to be based on the fear that he is endangered. The ingrained conviction that biological survival in the face of danger is the ultimate justification makes "self-defense" a nearly universally accepted moral explanation of violent behavior. Even flagrantly imperialistic or grandiose military campaigns such as, for example, Hitler's, begin with self-pitying rationalizations for the need of "Lebensraum" and preemptive strikes.

We have advanced the argument that the self which must be defended cannot be defined from without. It is uniquely defined, whether consciously or unconsciously, by a people itself. The extended self is not only coextensive with a people's land and physical assets, but also includes internalized belief systems and identifications based in history, culture, institutions, and the like. In psychoanalytic terms, people have different psychological sets of object representations and these differences make possible totally different,

APPENDIX

Self-Involvement with national territory: reflections of Israeli and Arab students at U.S. universities

Historically, much of the substance of international relations—interaction between sovereign states—has involved geographic issues. Questions of territory and boundaries are almost invariably involved in wars between nations. This Appendix reports a systematic exploration of the geographical concepts and emotional investment in the physical landscape as reflected by a sample of individuals who are citizens of several nations involved in the Arab-Israeli conflict.

Our subjects were students from the Middle East enrolled in graduate studies at several American universities. Like Youssef, (see Chapter 3), they invariably expressed profound commitments to specific geographic features and boundaries of their land which were widely shared by others from their countries. While some of these commitments were rationalized in military or economic terms, others evoked vigorous personal feelings whose quality and intensity far exceeded rational or realistic considerations. Consequently, the hypothesis which has evolved from this exploration is that such features of the land have become incorporated in the extended self of individuals.

As will be seen, self-involvement with the land represents a powerful determinant of perceptions and feelings which underpin decision and action with respect to territorial conflicts, and the quality and degree of such involvement can be determined only from individual participants.

During the period July 1972 through May 1973, a group of ten Arab and eight Israeli male graduate students attending universities in the Northeastern United States were interviewed in depth by one member of the Committee. All of the Israeli subjects had seen military service, as had two of the Arab students.

All these students showed a high degree of political sophistication and a thorough knowledge of the diplomatic-historical context of the Mideast. All of them could speak with a high degree of sophistication about the complexities of topics such as patron-client relations in international relations, strategic nodal points, policy statements designed for internal consumption as contrasted with external influence, and the kinds of problems faced by a nation incorporating a large unassimilated minority. These students, both Israelis and Arabs, were fully aware of various British-French zonal agreements of fifty years ago, some secret at the time, involving Turkey, Syria, Lebanon, Palestine, Iraq and Jordan. With respect to the contemporary international climate, none of the Israeli students feared an externally imposed territorial demarcation by the great powers; but all Arab students expressed this concern, referring in these terms to the United States and the Soviet Union.

The Israeli Students

All eight Israeli students firmly maintained the conviction that Jews had lived in "Israel" uninterruptedly for the past 4,000 years. They pointed out that Jews had lived in Palestine throughout the period of Turkish rule, and that Jews had both purchased land and improved the land during the British Mandate. Having asserted these views on residence, ownership, and development of the land, Israeli students would state or imply contempt toward the Arabs for not having improved the land. At the same time, the Israelis revealed a mystique for or identification with the land. For these Israeli students, tenancy of the land had taken on not just a legalistic legitimacy, but an overtone of moral righteousness.

Israeli students interviewed prior to October 1973 had developed an attitude toward Israeli society at that time that might most accurately be defined as a garrison mentality. That is, they perceived Israel as threatened on all sides and were convinced that a credo of pragmatic self-reliance was the essential factor that would see them through. While this conviction seemed to be characteristic of all the Israeli students, there were other more complex and conflictual issues affecting the internal stability of Israeli society. For example, each of the Israeli students was troubled by his perception that Israel, a nation founded as a haven for the dispossessed and persecuted, had itself occasioned hundreds of thousands of people, the Palestine Arabs, to be dispossessed. In the fall of 1972, this sympathy of Israeli toward Arab was greatly decreased by Palestinian guerilla acts of terrorism, the assassination of Israeli athletes at the Olympic Games in Germany, and incidents of aircraft hijacking.

The Israeli students interviewed prior to the October War of 1973 reflected a somewhat clearer view of what certain Arab nations *are not* than what Israel *is*. For example, several Israeli students were quite firm in their conviction that Egypt as a nation state, despite the "British-imposed" boundaries, had never really existed farther eastward than a north-south line at El Arish. One Israeli declared that there was no historical reason for the existence of Jordan and grandly stated that "The British liked geographic terms. There was a 'cis-Jordan' (Palestine), so there had to be a 'trans-Jordan' (Jordan). Actually, on a historical basis Jordan should simply be a province of Saudi Arabia." The same individual, however, was quick to contend that, "History aside, it is of the utmost importance to Israel that Jordan and Lebanon survive roughly as they are." All the Israeli students viewed both Iraq and Syria as governed by extremist regimes, and all expressed some fear that the two nations might join, citing the ill-fated attempt of the 1960's. Geographically, the Israeli students thought of Israel as an oasis or an outpost of civilization and science among the underdeveloped. They also viewed Israel as a land bridge vaguely connecting industrialized North America-Western Europe with India and the Far East, especially Japan. That is, the Israelis quite distinctly did not perceive of themselves as part of the "third world" and would object to attempts to so categorize them; they would consider it both inaccurate and demeaning. With respect to Israel as a geographic entity, Israeli students consistently emphasized the crucial importance of "defensible borders." Some of them stressed particularly the strategic advantages of water or mountain barriers, shortened border mileage, interior lines within those borders, and increased distance between population centers and borders. Israeli students held the view that time was on the side of Israel in that accomplished facts can eventually become legal realities.

This group of young men felt very strongly that if threatened, Israel would do "all that was required in order to survive," considering a hypothetical "worst-case" crisis situation confronting Israel. Most of these Israelis conceived of it in terms of what might result from not yet evidenced Arab unity in combination with Soviet support in varying degree, and compounded by American neglect. Given such a hypothetical situation, these students envisaged Israel becoming transformed into an enclave facing the sea in the form of a rectangle extending from Haifa to Janin to Nabulus to Jerusalem to Hebron to Gaza. Their rationale was that this configuration would allow Israel to maintain the territorial integrity of Tel Aviv and Jerusalem, and would permit Israeli forces to secure a defensible line alone the north-south mountain ridge comprising the Janin-Nabulus-Jerusalem-Hebron line. This "fall-back enclave," it should be noted, would include the western half of the West Bank. All Israeli students repeatedly stated that from this enclave Israel would seek to extend its territory and control at least to the Lebanese border, retake the Golan Heights and the Negev, and retake the Sinai westward to El Arish and southward to Sharm el Sheikh.

The Israeli students had devoted much less thought to the dimensions of a "best-case" situation than its opposite. Notions about an optimal situation for Israel were vague and ill-defined. However, certain features were commonly identified, along with the caveat that optimal conditions were unlikely to become reality. Features most often mentioned were:

1) Geography and political boundaries would remain as they were then (before October 1973), including an Israeli presence on the east bank of the Suez and at least the western half of the West Bank of the Jordan River.

2) All adjacent Arab states—Egypt, Lebanon, Jordan, Syria, and possibly Iraq as well, would accept Israeli technology and "know-how," with Israel maintaining a technological primacy in the Middle East. The internal contradictions in this scheme were seemingly not apparent to these Israeli students. Lebanon would be strongly supported, on the grounds that the continued existence of a Moslem-Christian state would benefit Israel. Jordan might be offered "privileges" (not rights) of access or transit of goods to the Mediterranean Sea. The Israeli students were more pessimistic about Israeli relations with Egypt, Syria, Iran and Libya.

The Arab Students

The Arab student informants, regardless of nationality, did not view Jewish residence in Palestine as having been established over 4,000 years of history. On the contrary, they viewed Jewish settlement as having been a minor factor, beginning in 1900 and becoming accelerated after 1945 to the point that it was regarded first as a source of irritation, then of anxiety and fear, until it ultimately represented a traumatic intrusion in their natural territory. That is, the Arab students unanimously considered the Jewish state in Palestine to be a European enclave forced upon them at their expense by other Europeans. They held the view that European Jews expropriated Arab land and displaced Arab people with the overt and covert support of other Europeans and subsequently of Americans and Russians, all of whom were acting from a sense of guilt engendered by the events of World War II. Unlike the Israeli students, these Arab students feared externally-imposed territorial solutions at Arab expense, specifically citing their apprehensions about Soviet-American collusion.

A constant theme of the Arab students was their fear of Israeli expansion. In their view, rising immigration of Russian and American Jews would diminish Israeli caution with respect to the Palestinian Arab population living within Israeli-held territory, would encourage Israel to hold to the 1967 truce boundaries, and could generate pressure within Israeli society for further territorial expansion. In support of this contention, eight of the Arab students cited the statement on "Zionist territorial requirements" of a viable Jewish state, published in 1918. They were quick to point out that this plan considered an integral part of Lebanon between the Israeli-Lebanese border and the Litani River (roughly the southern one-third of Lebanon) to be vital for water resource needs of the proposed Jewish state. They cited the same source as advocating that the Jewish state in Palestine be extended beyond the Jordan River to approximately 50 miles eastward along the Hejaz Railroad between Dera's and Ma'an, an integral part of Jordan.

With respect to Arab territorial aspirations, the more messianic of the Arab students envisaged an Arab nation stretching from

Mauritania, Morocco, Algeria, Libya, Egypt and Sudan in North Africa through the Arabian Peninsula, Palestine, Syria and Iraq. Even these idealists, however, did not advocate the annihilation of Israel, but indicated that their plan could accommodate a much reduced Jewish enclave centered at Tel Aviv, the extent of which remained vague. The implication was quite clear, however, that the smaller such an enclave, the better.

The majority of these students held the view that Arab unity, however desirable, must allow for regional differences; and each felt that a transitional stage in which the Arab world might federate into four regions was both possible and desirable. The four regions they identified were Mahgreb (North Africa), Syria-Iraq, the Arabian Peninsula, and the Nile Valley-Jordan Valley area consisting of Egypt-Sinai-Palestine-Jordan. Israel, as presently constituted, was regarded as a permanent "wedge" between the Nile Valley and Jerusalem-Jordan Valley. The common denominator in their view was that while the northern one-third to one-half of the former Palestine Mandate might remain a Jewish state, the southern half should be incorporated into an Egyptian-Jordanian juridical region of contiguous Arab territory. The extent to which a truncated Israeli state extending along the coast from Tel Aviv to the Lebanese border might be allowed to project eastward was vague, with opinion varying from student to student.

Two Palestinian Arabs who had grown up in refugee camps demonstrated the totalistic hatred and inclination toward violence described in people who have been deprived of power and self-esteem, that is, the characteristics of narcissistic rage. One of them described this feeling: "We have nothing, no land, no nation, no voice, no family—we are the living dead. As we die, we shall kill as many of our killers as we can."

Two other Palestinian Arabs from the Israeli-occupied West Bank demonstrated much ambivalence and conflict. While they were generally sympathetic to their extremist Jordanian fellow students, their perception of Israelis was less stereotypic. They expressed envy and admiration for Israeli technology and administrative skills, while adhering to a militant Arab ideology. For each, the contact with Israeli authorities had been quite personal in that parents had been allowed to retain property, and in one case a father had been encouraged to retain his position of administrative authority. One spoke with a grudging admiration of Israeli land reclamation: "The Jews restored the land. We must admit it; we neglected what was ours and what we want most." The other commented, "Yes, our standard of living is higher; yes, we have more money because of the Israelis—but we are eunuchs because of the Israelis."

Overall, the group of Arab students interviewed in 1973 held the same views of history and geography as had their colleagues who were interviewed one year earlier, with the exception that they seemed to have a much more ideological outlook, accompanied by a markedly diminished cosmopolitan attitude as compared to their colleagues of the previous year.

The October 1973 War: Israeli Views

Four Israeli students interviewed in early fall (pre-October) 1973 generally agreed on points of history and geography with the group of Israelis interviewed a year earlier. The second group did, however, differ to some extent with the first in that they were all raised on kibbutzim, had achieved junior officer rank, and had been in combat on at least one occasion. Each somewhat amusedly related that Israel was indeed a nation of many factions; and that Zionist ideologues, Eastern European Jews, and "Eastern Jews" (that is, dark-complexioned Jews from North Africa and the Middle East) were all viewed with varying degrees of disfavor on the grounds that they were alleged to be passive and non-pragmatic. Each of these young men felt strong affection for the Israeli military, which they considered to be not just a defense force, but also an agent of social change, a social organizer. Each was convinced that Israelis who were not raised on kibbutzim benefited greatly from their experience in the Israeli military forces. As far as these four Israelis were concerned, the Israeli army produced desirable changes in attitude and provided necessary basic skills for those who lacked them.

It is no exaggeration to state that these four Israeli students had a strong group adherence through the process of progressive stages of self identification with both societal and political institutions of their country. The sequence of extended self identification proceeded from kibbutz, to army, to nation state. Underlying this process of self identification ran a pervasive theme: the mystique of the land. Two of the Israeli students talked freely and knowledgeably about the history of the Israeli military forces, geopolitical and cultural factors, and political objectives. They stressed the historical tradition of the Israeli military, the identification with the land, and the notion of the underdog overcoming all odds. They related with obvious pride that recruits to the Israeli army assigned to tank units swear allegiance on the Masada Hills with the vow, "Masada will never fall again." Great emphasis is placed on the inter-relationship of history and the land. With a bristling pride they further note that in 1921 the Israeli defense force (the Haganah), while having no legal status, succeeded in defending Jewish settlements at Hebron against terrorist attacks ordered by the Grand Mufti of Jerusalem. At the same time, other Jewish settlements under British protection were apparently destroyed. Continuing on this theme, they pointed out that in 1940 Captain Wingate of the British Army became the commander of Jewish territorial forces. This is the same eccentric and mystical Wingate who nurtured a mystique of guerrilla warfare, and who later achieved fame in the British-Japanese conflict in Burma. It was from this military force commanded originally by Wingate that Jewish commando units were formed, known as the Palmach. Most highranking officers of the Israeli army (Zahal) were originally members of the Palmach. Not surprisingly, the Israeli students evaded discussion of dissident commando groups such as the Irgun and Stern units.

The Israeli students repeatedly and correctly insisted that prior to June, 1967, Israel consisted of a narrow strip of territory approximately 265 miles long, but with 595 miles of frontier. At Elat on the Gulf of Aqaba the coastline extended only 6 miles. Tel Aviv was 12 miles from the Jordanian border, and Jerusalem was at the point of a salient 12 miles wide.

After 1967, they observed, Israel had 312 miles of frontier to defend, and despite a failure to achieve strategic depth, there was a distance of some 44 miles between Tel Aviv and Jordan rather than 12, and 150 miles between Egyptian forces to the west of the Suez Canal and Elat rather than a theoretical distance of zero. Clearly, our student subjects were attempting to expand their territorial extended self commitment to coincide with national strategic considerations, attempting to convince themselves as well as the interviewer.

Israeli military training is unique. The Israeli army exerts an influence over all Israeli male citizens from age 14 to age 50. The importance of the Israeli army as a generator of societal cohesion cannot be over-emphasized. The army organizes instruction to bring all recruits up to a standard level of educational and cultural achievement. For the officers, a stated objective is that each should be a "fighting intellectual." Field grade officers (with a rank of major and upward) must have a university education, which may be subsidized by the army. At higher ranks of the military hierarchy "Eastern" Jews are notably absent; few have achieved the educational level required. While an elite officer corps is nurtured and fostered, it must be stressed that the trappings of such a corps are markedly absent. Food for officers and men is the same. All ranks eat at the same tables. Uniforms for officers and ranks are the same and free of plumage and polish. Israeli army training, while striving to inculcate tactical expertise in every soldier, may well produce an additional bonus. For approximately 18 months, each Israeli soldier goes on maneuvers all over Israel. At each locale recruits study topographical and geological maps, history of the region, plans for its development, key points for military tactics, and lines of communication. At each locale the recruit is exposed to its paths, villages, caves, hills, roads, and gorges by means of long route marches and by films. Clearly, this training achieves more than its surface aim of developing tactical skills among recruits.

By physical and visual contact with the earth and the land, Israeli soldiers are encouraged to form extended self identifications with the non-human environment. This intense and intimate exposure to the land, achieved under the sound rationale of thorough tactical training, appears to engender psychological changes in many recruits, in that aspects of the land acquire properties of a self-object. That is, aspects of external geography and topography are to some extent invested with narcissistic energy, and become treated as part of the self. To the extent that this process does in fact occur, such soldiers become intensely committed to territorial integrity and its defense. However, while they recognized this quality in Israeli soldiers, the Israeli students did not consider it to be even a remote possibility that Egyptian or Syrian soldiers might develop similar and equally strong identifications. They did feel, though, that Palestine Arabs might possess similar geographic attachment, to judge from the vigor with which such a possibility was rejected.

The emotional attachment of Israelis to the land, the mystique of the land, seemed to derive from three sources. Firstly, Israelis have developed an almost religious credo of improving or restoring the land. This credo has been reinforced in a very concrete and personalized way during their military service by their intimate knowledge and familiarity with the terrain in many parts of the country and its occupied territories. Secondly, a great many Israeli men have shared profound experiences in certain regions and places within that territory. Thirdly, it is part of their positive self-image to own and possess land and avoid the negative ego-ideal of the homeless and wandering Jew.

Since there have been so many wars in so few years (1948, 1956, 1967, 1973), and since each adult Israeli male is a citizen-soldier, it follows that there are many Israelis who have fought at a given locale more than once. Furthermore, a great many others who have not fought at a given place themselves have had older brothers or fathers who have done so just a few years earlier. An intense emotional attachment to the land is fostered by such experience of shared intimacy. For example, for a farmer who has been subject to artillery shelling by the Syrian army from the Golan Heights, and for his son who grew up exposed to that everyday reality and who as a young soldier took part in the assault on the Golan Heights, that particular piece of terrain becomes, psychologically, much more than topography. If fathers, uncles, and older brothers were at key points in the Sinai in 1956 and 1967, and if their sons in 1973 were again at key points along the ridge line forty miles east of the Suez Canal, sites such as the Mitla Pass and Gidi Pass may become invested with deeper emotional attachment than they might appear to be worth strategically.

Since the Israelis have had a high rate of exposure to combat with a relatively low casualty rate, the proportion of veterans with emotionally charged memories is high. And since in the Egyptian and Syrian armies the number who have been exposed to combat has been a relatively small proportion of the total population, while their casualty rates have been disproportionately high, this same psychological phenomenon among Arab veterans is likely to be considerably less evident.

In considering this psychological phenomenon of intense emotional attachment to terrain, we must also point out that a striking irony has been at work. While the Arabs have launched several military actions intended to reclaim Arab land, the very number of their military initiatives have served to increase the numbers of Israeli men who have experienced intense emotions at key points on that land. These Israelis have become less and less inclined to yield. At the same time, the frustration of those repeated Arab efforts to force Israeli withdrawal from occupied Arab lands has bred more and more younger Arabs determined to reverse previous military humiliations and redeem Arab pride. As a consequence, emotionally highly invested symbols, cognitive maps and terrain have become far more than geopolitical factors. They have become fused with the self, extensions of the self, which may properly be conceptualized as extended self identifications.

We feel strongly that this series of interviews with Arab and Israeli graduate students has demonstrated the central importance of the intense emotional attachment to land regarded as theirs. Psychological investment of the land appears to have sprung from (among other sources) shared experiences of daily life associated with specific locales—from shared experience of planting and construction, of marriages, births and burials. Intensity of feeling for the land has been inculcated, or further enhanced, by practical training and by oral teaching. Much of this has been accomplished by military experience. This extension of the self to include the psychological representation of physical features of the land may be paralleled at the cognitive level by the development of internal maps.

This investigation has, we believe, pointed up the probable instability, perhaps inviability, of any territorial settlement which does not take into account the needs of both Israelis and Palestinians for continuing their emotional attachment to at least some of their original land base.

ACKNOWLEDGMENTS TO CONTRIBUTORS

The program of the Group for the Advancement of Psychiatry, a nonprofit, tax exempt organization, is made possible largely through the voluntary contributions and efforts of its members. For their financial assistance during the past fiscal year in helping it to fulfill its aims, GAP is grateful to the following:

Abbott Laboratories
Maurice Falk Medical Fund
Geigy Pharmaceuticals
Mrs. Carol Gold
The Gralnick Foundation
The Grove School
The Holzheimer Fund
Ittleson Foundation, Inc., for the Blanche F. Ittleson Consultation Program
Lederle Laboratories
Merck, Sharp & Dohme Laboratories
The Phillips Foundation
Roche Laboratories
Sandoz Pharmaceuticals
Schering-Plough Corporation
The Murray L. Silberstein Fund (Mrs. Alan H. Kalmus)
Smith Kline & French Laboratories
van Ameringen Foundation
Leo S. Weil Foundation
Wyeth Laboratories

OTHER RECENT PUBLICATIONS
GROUP FOR THE ADVANCEMENT OF PSYCHIATRY

No.	Title	Price
102	THE CHRONIC MENTAL PATIENT IN THE COMMUNITY	$3.50
101	POWER AND AUTHORITY IN ADOLESCENCE: THE ORIGINS AND RESOLUTIONS OF INTERGENERATIONAL CONFLICT	6.50
100	PSYCHOTHERAPY AND ITS FINANCIAL FEASIBILITY WITHIN THE NATIONAL HEALTH CARE SYSTEM	2.50
99	WHAT PRICE COMPENSATION?	2.50
98	PSYCHIATRY AND SEX PSYCHOPATH LEGISLATION: THE 30s TO THE 80s	4.00
97	MYSTICISM: SPIRITUAL QUEST OR PSYCHIC DISORDER?	4.00
96	RECERTIFICATION: A LOOK AT THE ISSUES	2.50

Orders amounting to less than $5.00 must be accompanied by remittance. All prices are subject to change without notice.

GAP publications may be ordered on a subscription basis. The current subscription cycle comprising the Volume X Series covers the period from July 1, 1977 to June 30, 1980. For further information, write the Publications Office (see below).

Bound volumes of GAP publications issued since 1947 are also available which include GAP titles no longer in print and no longer available in any other form. A bound index of volumes (I through VII) has been published separately.

Please send your order and remittance to: Publications Office, Group for the Advancement of Psychiatry, 419 Park Avenue South, New York, New York 10016.

This publication was produced for the Group for the Advancement of Psychiatry by the Mental Health Materials Center, Inc., New York